ARNSIDE

A Guide and Community History
from 1800 to the present day

Written by Dennis Bradbury

and illustrated with further photographs from his Arnside Archive

Table of Contents

Page	
1	A Guide and Community History
2	Introduction
5	Arnside Life
10	Arnside Village and Parish 2002 (Map)
11	Eastern Approaches
12	*The Hincaster Branch Line*
16	The River Kent Front
17	*Arnside Railway Viaduct*
23	The Centre Front Shops
28	Church Hill, Church and Chapel
30	*The Crossfields of Arnside*
32	*Arnside Educational Institute*
34	*Robert Gibson, Yeoman Farmer and Methodist Preacher*
39	Silverdale Road and Top o' the Hill
43	The West Promenade and Beachwood Beach
47	*Earnseat Boarding School for Boys*
50	*Ashmeadow House*
53	*The Boat-Builder Crossfields (1838-1951)*
57	Red Hills
57	*Oakfield School 1884-1959*
65	Upper Silverdale Road, the Tower and Far Arnside
73	Arnside Knott and New Barns
74	*The Convalescent Home*
Encovers	1862 and 2002 village maps

ARNSIDE

A Guide and Community History

A Second Look

The revised narrative of this, the Queen's Golden Jubilee Year Edition of my guide to Arnside, does not claim to result from a much greater depth of research. It stems more from a continued reading and study of the more readily available documents, photographs, postcards and maps of Arnside. Responses to the First Edition, both verbal and written, have been very helpful. As before, more information of the 20th century has been gleaned by talking to longer-established residents of the village. Some points must still remain largely speculative and open to correction by those with greater knowledge than my own. Readers of the previous edition will note that there are some further factual alterations made as more evidence has been brought to my notice. Much additional material has been inserted and the original photographs have been changed for a new set that hopefully will be of equal interest.

This booklet is an attempt to record something of the village history of the last two centuries while, largely, remaining a descriptive introduction to Arnside. It is based on the original walk format of my first publication - 'A Walk Around Arnside', now long out of print. As a guide the map will help with orientation and permit a start anywhere in the narrative.

It is obvious from my conversations and enquiries that much valuable, historical information remains hidden, put aside or temporarily lost in boxes, drawers, attics and lofts. My 'Arnside Archive' is an attempt to accumulate all existing historical records, in any and all formats, with a view to placing copies, or originals, in the Kendal Record Office for the benefit of the generations to follow. To this end I would be pleased to hear of any collections of news cuttings, photographs, slides or other ephemera relating, especially, to the period 1800 to 1980 that bring to light information not included, or hinted at, in this present publication. I would be particularly interested to see material relating to the several private schools that receive mention but little detail.

I hope that you will consider your purchase of this little volume to be your 'Catch of the Day'!

Catch of the day in 1904

INTRODUCTION

Arnside, as a substantial village, is not very old, going back little more than a hundred and fifty years. The construction of the railway and the consequent improvement of the roads, in this remote southern corner of Westmorland, were the spurs to its development. Before 1800, the majority of the population, of the Arnside portion of Beetham Parish, lived to the south of Arnside Knott, the lumpy hill behind the present-day village. This is the area, well known to many caravanners, originally the hamlet of Heathwaite, but now referred to as Far Arnside. Within what was to become the present Arnside Civil Parish, there were only about 120 people, living in some 25 dwellings. Most would be involved with farming, inn-keeping, fishing or, to a lesser extent, other craft trades such as builder, quarry worker, stonemason, carpenter, joiner, leather-worker or blacksmith. Most of the land, prior to 1800, was in the hands of two farming families - the Sauls and the Burrows (also recorded as Borrows). This ownership was to change at the beginning of the 19th century when these lands were bought, largely, by the Wilsons of Dallam Tower and the Barkers of 'Saltcotes'. The farmers were to remain as tenants.

As a coastal settlement alongside a navigable estuary, there was also involvement with shipping and boat building. It should be noted that Milnthorpe, higher up the estuary at the mouth of the River Bela, was the only port of Westmorland. Grange and the western shore were then in Lancashire. Although shipping would ply up and down the river to Milnthorpe, there were other quays and anchorages, such as Sandside and Arnside, down-river towards Silverdale. In the 18th and early 19th centuries, the ships would bring iron ore, agricultural products, building timber, coal, tar, salt, white lead for paint and linseed oil for putty, grains, potatoes, and tobacco. They would carry away quarry stone and finished goods such as gunpowder, cloth and snuff from Kendal and surrounding areas. In yet earlier times, as we shall see, salt was won from the sea and sent elsewhere. The coastal craft would carry goods around the Irish Sea and the Cumbrian coast to and from other ports such as Liverpool, Whitehaven, Workington, Belfast and Dublin.

Arnside remained as a small, scattered hamlet on the southern fringe of Westmorland, and Beetham Parish, until the middle of the nineteenth century. Parish records indicate a little movement of the population but, on the whole, numbers remained fairly static. Any new building merely replaced that which had become uninhabitable or no longer needed. Approaches to Arnside were simply tracks and bridleways. There were tracks to Beetham through Leighton Beck, with its iron furnace, and through Sandside by the coastal 'sands' route. A bridleway went over The Knott to Arnside Tower farm and on to Silverdale. The nearest turnpike road could be joined at Leighton Beck. This road, from Warton and on to Beetham, Milnthorpe and Kendal, was then one of the two main routes to the north, the other going via Burton-in-Kendal. There would have been lesser tracks connecting the various farms at Arnside Tower, Arnside Well,

Ashmeadow House in 1908

'Hollins', New Barns, 'Lawrence House', 'Saltcotes' and Black Dyke plus shoreside inns at 'The Fighting Cocks' and on the sites of present-day 'Ashmeadow' and 'Beachwood'.

Reasons for change in the early nineteenth century are uncertain, but as Far Arnside declined and houses were deserted, so the present-day village began to grow on the northern slopes of The Knott. The building of the railway in the 1850s accelerated the process. A few wealthy merchants, solicitors, bankers and ship owners bought and enlarged some of the existing, more cottage-type properties, such as those at 'Beachwood' and 'Ashmeadow'. Others built substantial new dwellings such as 'Wood Close' (c.1802), 'Greenwood House' (now The Albion Hotel) (c.1810), and 'Morecambe Cottage' (now 'Springfield House') (c.1820).

Most significant 'off-comers', around 1818, were the Crossfield family. John Crossfield, a boat builder and repairer originally from the Ulverston area, moved to Arnside from Milnthorpe. His two young sons, Thomas and Francis, were apprenticed in Lancaster as carpenters. John set up in business as a lath cleaver, carpenter and probably barrel maker for the estuary shipping trade, utilising the coppice wood that then covered much of The Knott. The sons soon joined the business. In the late 1830s, the Crossfields began building small boats. From such beginnings the boat building business was to flourish for over 100 years down the generations. We shall see how these individuals, and their descendants among others, were to have a profound influence on the development of Arnside as a true village community.

4

Arnside Front in 1908

The building of the railway and the estuary viaduct, between 1853 and 1857, really put Arnside on the map. By chance, this event coincided with the land survey for the publication of the first, 1860, large-scale Ordnance Maps of Westmorland. The railway is shown in its original single-track form. The population numbers, fairly static until mid-century, now began to increase. About 150 in 1850; 200 in 1870; 550 in 1890; the population had risen to some 850 souls, in 180 dwellings, by 1900. In 2002, the population is estimated to be some 2400 people in 1160 dwellings. Arnside has come a long way in 150 years, being now one of the most highly populated villages in South Lakeland though quite a few of its dwellings are holiday homes not in full-time occupation.

By 1905 Arnside was not only regarded as Westmorland's only 'seaside' holiday resort; with Bed & Breakfast accommodation, a few shops and beautiful situation; but also as a pleasant place to live if you worked in Kendal or anywhere else easily accessible by rail.

I can do no better than to quote from a, century-old, guide to Arnside to note what it was like at the start of the 20th century.

"The village is truly a seat of quietude and natural loveliness, a source of great health and the radiating point of charmingly picturesque drives. The botanist finds his heaven in the great variety of wild flowers and plants. The striking profusion of daffodils and lilies of the valley is a remarkable feature of the village, growing not by twos and threes but by acres, in their seasons.

Boating and fishing are the principal pastimes. Accommodation is excellent in every way and good apartments, in cheery parts, are easy to secure, excepting in the height of the season in August. Arnside is very free of the rough element and its stillness is not even interrupted by a band. It is singularly the home for a month's

quiet recuperation so necessary to the average business mind subject to the tension and extreme pressure of the age. The sandy shore is the field for children and right heartily do they avail themselves of its advantages.

It looks very pretty with its villas and cottages dotted about in the fashion of supreme watering place irregularity. Some are built on jutting crags and, seemingly, in out of the way places, while others are situated by the shore or among the narrow winding roads everywhere romantic and rich in picturesque combinations."

Almost continuous development, on both large and small scales, has continued. Silverdale Road developed, basically from the bottom upwards, filling in most of the available spaces. Only the Memorial Playing Field (Big King) and the Council allotments have survived. The 1920s and 1930s saw further developments of Church Hill, Orchard Road, New Barns, Black Dyke Road, Redhills Road and High Knott Road. The greatest expansion followed the Second World War with the development of the Plantation and Swinnate estates and the council estates of Kings Close, Queens Drive and Stewart Close. Final phases of 20th century development were The Inglemeres, The Spinney area, Parkside and Lawrence Drives, Ashleigh Court and The Meadows together with a number of conversions and in-fill buildings such as those at 'Heathcliffe' (1991) and 'Wood Close' (2000). Biggest change in 2002, at the start of the new millennium, has been the demolition of Grange View Convalescent Home, built in 1939, and its replacement by the even larger block of superior apartments, 'The Grange'.

The village is a vital and important part of the Arnside/Silverdale Area of Outstanding Natural Beauty, designated in 1972. Only some 75 sq.km. in area, with 30 sq.km. of intertidal, estuary shoreline, the A.O.N.B. straddles the Cumbria/Lancashire counties' boundary. One of the smallest As.O.N.B. it is remarkable for its great variety of landscape topography, geological features, flora and fauna. Arnside has become particularly attractive to the South Lakeland visitor as one of the few points where the tidal waters of the Kent Estuary, with its abundant bird life, mountain back-drop, and beautiful sunsets, can easily be seen.

ARNSIDE LIFE

Up to the end of the Second World War in 1945 Arnside remained very much a rural community with, then, a population of about 1,200 in 350 dwellings. Surrounded by the River Kent to the north and farmland on all other sides, there was little of an urban character apart from an unusual number of large individual, semi-detached and terraced houses. In general these were associated with wealthy Barrow, Kendal and Lancaster commuters or with tourist trade guesthouses, dating from the 1880s. In the early years of the 20th century the village was base for four large (in rural terms) boarding schools, and several lesser, private schools, all occupying, or expanded on, such residences. In this period the pupil population would probably have been equivalent to some 20% of the resident population. In the 1920s and 30s we can add to this the floating, visitor population, in various types of accommodation. Judging

The Kent estuary and rail viaduct

by the fact that an address list offered some 60 providers of self-catering or bed and breakfast facilities in the 1920s, one can imagine that the village population could temporarily double in the holiday season.

The attractions were obvious. A tidal estuary with attractive, if not particularly sandy, beaches; country walks in a relatively uncommon limestone area with a variety of flora and fauna to match; and opportunities for fishing, sailing, coach outings or trips around the bay. Arnside was, of course, the only seaside resort of Westmorland on its small, 6 km. shoreline from Milnthorpe to the counties' boundary at Far Arnside. In its heyday it was possible to identify some 36 shops and commercial outlets serving a resident population of about 1,500 in 240 dwellings. This was the period when all larger houses employed a number of servants.

A record of 1965 indicates that the village then had 787 dwellings, 500 static caravans, 32 shops, 6 cafés, 7 farms, 2 garages, 2 hotels, 4 guesthouses, 2 pubs, 2 banks, 4 schools, and 2 meeting halls. Today we can find only some 25 businesses serving about 1200 dwellings. Now the floating, resident population is almost nil as there are probably fewer than ten places able to offer accommodation. Arnside is now largely a place for the day visitor indulging in similar interests to their forebears.

Crossfield-built boats in 1904

Though a relatively small community in much of the 20th century, the village was not backward in its provision of social, sporting, educational and religious interests in addition to attentions to the rural calendar. The latter concerned itself with ploughing competitions; hedging, walling and ditching; hunting, shooting and fishing; and harvest festivals. This carried over into the Women's Institute movement with talks, preserve making, cake making, garden parties and play-acting. In turn this led to the formation of drama groups and the Arnside Players who have regularly produced plays in the Village Hall or the Educational Institute since the 1930s. The latter forms part of the educational and social history of the village, originating in the 1880s and providing lecture and reading facilities in addition to exercise activities such as table tennis, badminton and snooker. It also continues to provide venues for debate, socials and dancing, political meetings, bridge and chess.

For a village, the range of societies is almost too numerous to mention. Few have been able to claim that Arnside is not the place for the mentally and/or physically active retired. The youth of the village are not forgotten. We can find a Brownie Group, Guide Company, Scout Group and Playgroup. Glancing at the local directory we may instance an Art Group, Bridge Club, Chess Club, Choral Society, Discussion Group, Horticultural Society, Natural History Society, and a Village Society. Proposals are currently in hand to form a youth council.

Coronation Tree Planting Ceremony 1953

The religious character of village life has been established by the three churches - the Parish Church of St. James (1866), the Robert Gibson Memorial Methodist Chapel (1876), and the Roman Catholic Chapel of Our Lady of Lourdes (1926). Quaker meetings were once held in the old Institute building in Pier Lane. At some time, there has been an active Boys Brigade, a Young Women's Christian Association Group, a Band of Hope and a TocH group. One of the boarding schools was a Wesleyan Methodist foundation from late in the 19th century.

Although small, the village has played its part in wartime, providing services personnel, nurses, fire fighters, home guard units and civil defence units, in the Boer War and the First and Second World Wars, with no small sacrifice of life. Memorial tablets can be seen in the Institute, in the churches and in the upper woodland walk of Ashmeadow. The civilian response was equally important and large sums of money were raised by a variety of funding efforts. Results were comforts in the First World War; cigarettes, tobacco and chocolate in the Second World War together with moneys for munitions, planes and tanks as National Savings and 'Wings for Victory' weeks. Additionally the Women's Royal Voluntary Service, originally the W.V.S. in the village, fabricated camouflage netting for the services and helped with civilian rationing and evacuees. Even the schools helped by 'digging for victory', keeping hens and tending beehives to produce honey. The Royal British Legion, including its Women's Section, has played, and continues to play, a significant role in village affairs. For many years it organised the village Summer Fete and Sports. It now organises the bi-annual car boot sales on the Memorial Field to raise money for disabled services pensioners and

'Paddlers All!' c.1908

Christmas gifts for the needy elderly of the village. George Smith and his wife, Ruby Smith MBE, are to be commended for their Legion work and unfailing efforts on behalf of the community in so many ways.

Arnside has never been lacking in its provision of sporting facilities and, where appropriate, the recruiting and training of competitive teams. In early days this may have taken the form of an inter-community ploughing competition or a sailing regatta. The 20th century has seen the introduction of football, cricket, tennis, badminton, table tennis, gymnastics, dancing, wild fowling, billiards, then snooker, and bowls. There are even several sections in the Ramblers' Group to suit all abilities from mountain scrambling to a riverside stroll. One might even include the, now defunct, brass band of the 1930s. Most activities have survived and flourished over the years to gain appropriate facilities. For a quarter of a century the multifarious activities of the village; from socials to sports, to meetings, to religious services; have been bound together by the 'Arnside Broadsheet'. Supported by donations, delivered to all residents and produced monthly by the efforts of a small team, this news sheet aims to make everyone aware of what is 'going on' in their own locality.

THE ARNSIDE 2002 BROADSHEET

ARNSIDE VILLAGE AND PARISH 2002

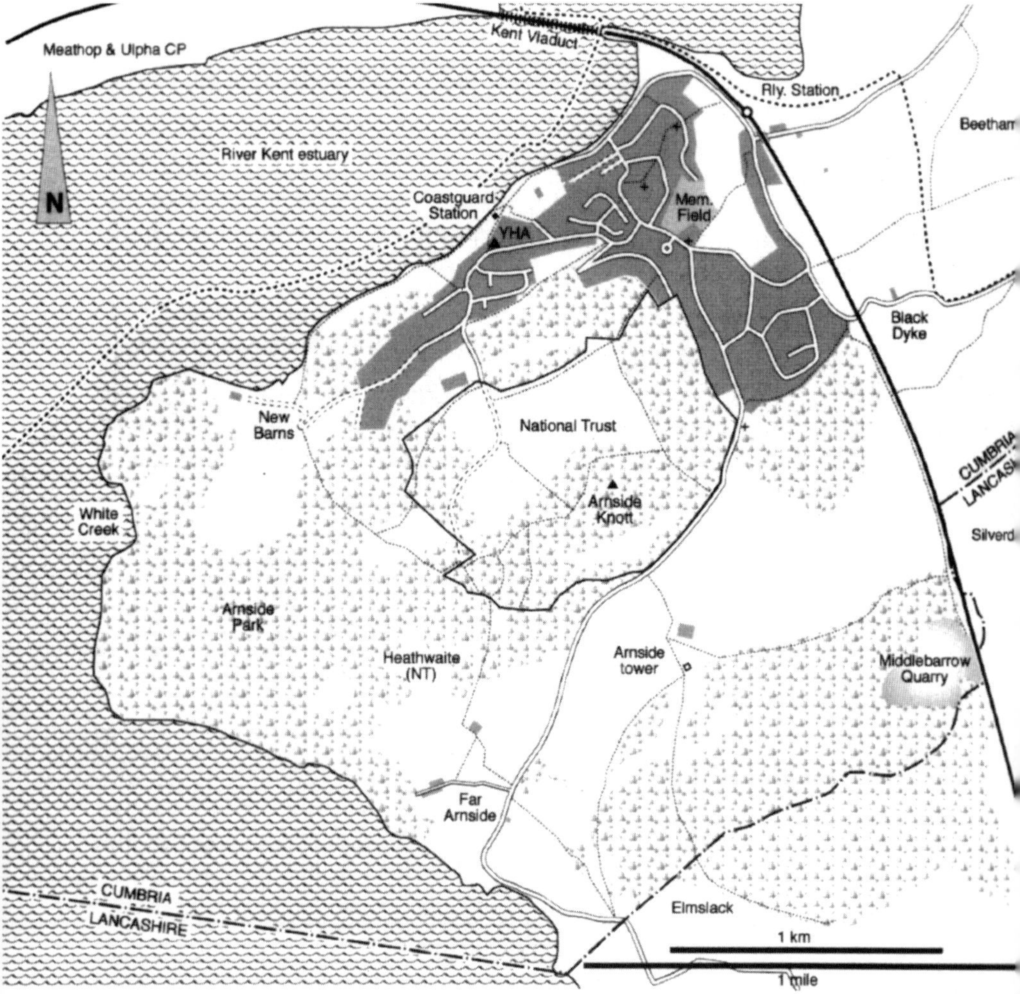

See inside rear cover for village maps

Eastern Approaches

The Civil Parish boundary is defined on the east by Leighton Beck, the main drain for the Arnside Mosses (or Marshes), passing under the Milnthorpe Road and the old railway embankment to join the River Kent. From here it runs parallel to the road until, reaching the viaduct, it runs out into the estuary. In its higher reaches the beck also marks the counties' boundary. Thus all the salt-marsh above the viaduct lies in the parish of Beetham. This salt-marsh area is used to produce lawn turf and, it is said, much of the material for the old (1926) Wembley Stadium was taken from here.

Facing Arnside Knott, the hill to the southwest that dominates Arnside, Arnside Mosses lie to the left. This area, now pastureland, was divided into strips, or turbaries. The hedges and dykes largely remain but turbary rights are no longer exercised here. Turbary rights allowed farmers, and others, to dig peat, as fuel, in their allotted strips. In early days, the marshes belonged to the Lords of the Manor of Beetham and, later, to the Wilsons of Dallam Tower. Few farmers actually owned this type of land and this is largely true even today.

In 1776, a group of local farmers got together money and materials to build a low dyke or embankment to prevent tidal flooding. This dyke, lying immediately to the inland side of the road, ran between the bottom slope of The Knott and the rise at Carr Bank, about a kilometre in all. It effectively allowed drainage and recovery of many acres of land in Arnside, Carr Bank and, inland, almost as far as Waterslack. It would have been breached many times by some of the exceptional high spring tides. Certainly this was the case in 1795 when the highest tides for over 50 years were experienced. Hereabouts, a dyke can refer either to an embankment or to a drainage ditch. Up to the middle of the nineteenth century, the railway embankment would not have been there and the sea would still have often flooded the marshes at the highest tides.

On the estuary side of the road are the remains of an old orchard, established by a village grocer, James Crossfield, in the nineteenth century. Through the trees can be seen a considerably higher embankment than that on the left. This is all that remains of a railway branch-line from Arnside to Hincaster, opened on the 26th June 1876. There was quite a substantial station platform and siding system to accommodate the single-line working and the advent of the quarry at Sandside. At Hincaster the branch joined the main line from Lancaster to Carlisle. The line gave access from the Barrow line to Kendal and the Lakes, via Oxenholme, and to County Durham, via Tebay. The prime purpose of this branch had been to make an easier connection, between the Durham coalfields and the Lancashire steelworks at Barrow and Millom. There were two intermediate stations, on the branch-line, at Sandside and Heversham. The completion of the railway to Carnforth, and the main line, had originally been at the instigation of the steelmasters of Furness for this same purpose. In the late nineteenth century and well into the twentieth century the branch line was to prove useful in the development and growth of the quarry at Sandside by greatly facilitating the movement of its quality, construction limestone. It is recorded that this quarry supplied the stone for the initial construction of Blackpool Promenade.

Hincaster Branch, Sandside Station c. 1912

The Hincaster Branch Line

It is doubtful whether the line's prime purpose was successful. Almost certainly, changes in steel production methods and the growth of the West Cumberland coalfields rendered the possibility uneconomic. Until closure, the line had been useful for Arnside, Storth and Heversham residents to reach Kendal, Carlisle, the Lakes via Windermere, and Scotland. Passenger services ceased in May 1942 and the through line was finally closed in September 1963. The Sandside viaduct, over the River Bela at Dallam, was demolished in 1966 and the remaining line, or siding, to Sandside quarry, was lifted in 1971. Part of this siding, behind Arnside Station, was used to accommodate the Royal Train when visits were being made to Holker Hall, or to other events in Cumbria. The last occasion was in March 1965. The embankment is a more effective tide barrier than that of 1776 but, even so, it was breached in the 1980s. Today while it remains part of the Dallam Estate it is a pleasant permissive walkway approached over the station steps.

This road here, Sandside Road, was provided by the railway company as a compensation road for the loss of access to the old shoreline 'sands' route to Sandside and to a track, which came across the moss from High Black Dyke Farm, to the south.

Nearer the railway, on the south side of the road, is a pair of semi-detached houses, built by Elijah Nelson in 1920 and where, it is said, some 5 metres of peat had to be dug out to reach a firm foundation. On the north side are another house and a bungalow roughly marking the site of the ill-fated gas-works, started in 1904 but never successfully completed. It went into liquidation in 1907. The house had been intended for the gas-works manager. Gas only came to Arnside in the 1970s with the arrival of piped natural gas. Here, now, a large gateway gives entry to a lorry yard, originally the site of railway sidings, a line-side crane, a coal yard and access to the old up-line railway station. For many years strident efforts have been made for the railway to retrieve this area for a rail car park as, currently, the right of public access for cars and taxis to the up-line platform is disputed. The next house, just before the bridge, was the station-master's but is no longer railway property as the station is now unstaffed. The dyke, or water drain, alongside the railway here, is the original Black Dyke that gave its name to Black Dyke Road on the other side of the railway. This drains the land below Tower Farm to the southwest.

Cyclists in Station Yard c. 1913

The railway bridge over the road, dating from 1912, replaced an earlier, narrow, 13 ft. wide, bridge, which in turn had replaced the original level crossing. The change required the creation of the lower road levels at this point and, most likely, coincided with the widening of Low Road to form Black Dyke Road. Passing under the railway bridge we find Black Dyke Road to the left and Station Road to the right.

Along Station Road, past the garage, are shop premises that, in the 1900s had been Mrs. Whinray's 'Oriental Café'. In the holiday heydays of the 1910s to 1930s, this was Christopher Shepherd's Grocery Shop and Café. Later still, this was to become the 'Wayside Coffee Bar'. Following a period of short-time occupations by various other businesses a hairdresser currently occupies it. Beyond here a public footpath divides the field on the left. This path is one of the oldest pedestrian rights of way in the village, effectively stretching to New Barns Farm and beyond. Land beneath the road, the railway and the bottom of the field, was the site of the old saltpans associated with the big house over to the left behind the garage.

The house was 'Saltcotes Hall', built in the 17th Century as a home and farmstead for a branch of the Saul family that probably came from High Black Dyke Farm or Leighton Beck Farm. A date-mark of 1679 is to be found in the house. The Sauls established a salt-cote wherein crude salt was produced by evaporation of the seawater that could flow into clay-lined troughs or 'pans', at suitable high tides. Most salt, an important dietary commodity, was produced by the evaporation process until the large-scale extraction of mineable 'rock salt' was established in the salt (-wich) towns of Cheshire around the mid-1700s. The tall window, at this side of the house, probably resulted from the imposition of the window tax of 1695. (The more windows, the more tax.) In the early 19th century the hall and farm were sold to the Burrows family and then, by marriage, passed to the Barkers. It remained in the hands of the Barkers and the Bradley-Barkers until well on into the 20th century. The Lancaster Gazette, in 1828, carries an advertisement from Robert Barker offering the property to let. It suggests that there were ten lodging rooms on the 2nd and 3rd floors 'convenient for

Saltcotes Hall Farm c. 1912

bathers'. Arnside must have been a health resort even at that time! In 1830 the Gazette records the accidental death of Mrs. Barker. Proceeding to Kendal market with a horse and cart, the cart turned over on to her and, fracturing her skull, killed her. In the twentieth century the estate and house have been occupied by a number of different families. This remains as one of the oldest inhabited dwellings in Arnside. Being involved with the estuary shipping trade, at the beginning of the eighteenth century, one of the barns was used for the storage of gunpowder from the mills at Sedgwick, near Kendal. 'Saltcotes' can still provide holiday cottage, letting accommodation.

The railway station building, on the south-bound side, is of little note being a replacement, of about 1914, for the 1859 original, which was a more-imposing, timber-framed building. Notable features, in Furness Railway days, would have been the wrought iron seats with the 'squirrel and grapes' logo of the Company, and the standard oil lamps, which, for economy, were extinguished between train arrivals. A stone station building of 1862 stood where the present concrete block shelter stands on the down-side, having been built to accommodate the, then, new double-line working. This had a booking office, waiting rooms, toilets, news and book-stall (before 1915) and even a refreshment room. The latter was run by the Bradley-Barkers of 'Saltcotes' in its day. Probably one of the most important items was the large station clock, which, in the 19th century, effectively determined Arnside's 'standard' time. For many years part of this building was used to house the stationmaster and his family. He was to be followed, in occupation, by platelayer Toby Lishman and his family when the new station house was built around 1906. At one period in the 1960s the Pearsons had a small ice-cream parlour, at the roadside, underneath the station. These buildings were finally demolished in 1986. The footbridge, originally with oil lamps, was a

Arnside Station and a Barrow train c. 1912

later addition of 1910. The platforms have been varied in length from time to time and partly raised to do away with the need for portable steps. The signal box is a 1906 replacement for the original 1860's box, which had resulted from the creation of the Hincaster Branch.

It is the railway itself, which is of some significance. It proved to be a prime factor in the development of the village. It improved access, in days before the advent of the internal combustion engine. The railway gave access to both north and south making commuting possible to Kendal, Lancaster, Barrow and even further afield. In its later days, the Barrow to Kendal train was affectionately referred to as 'Kendal Tommy'. Similarly, in railway parlance, the last train from Carnforth to Barrow was referred to as 'The Whip'. This name apparently derives from the term 'whipper-in' as some carriages, from the London to Scotland train, were slipped at Carnforth to be taken on to Barrow.

The remaining station building, on the up-line side, is, currently, the headquarters building of the Countryside Management Service for the Arnside/Silverdale Area of Outstanding Natural Beauty. The Area is defined by the bounds of the A6 trunk road and the Rivers Bela, Kent and Keer. The Countryside Management project was initiated in 1984 and, with its nucleus of permanent staff and volunteer helpers, seeks to look after the walls, paths, and signs of the AONB, together with management of woodlands, orchards, ponds and shoreline. It is administered through a Steering Committee and Landscape Trust that produces an admirable set of local guides and publishes an

Old Arnside Station building c. 1912

informative, quarterly, membership magazine 'Keer to Kent'. Some administration changes are anticipated as a result of the 'Countryside Rights of Way Act. 2000'. Visitors are very welcome at the far rear door of the building. Much useful information about the A.O.N.B. and a variety of walks can be obtained there, largely for free.

An incongruously large, block of modern flats lies at the end of the field. Until 1990 this was the site of Arnside Garage, established in the 1920s and incorporating the local wireless depot. The latter stocked 3, 4, 5, and even 7-valve radio receivers in 1928. Its advertisements of that period even claimed to provide receiver, remote control! For many years there were cattle pens at the side of the railway track opposite here. Before the advent of the railway, this was the point where the track from Arnside went across the sands to St. John's Cross at Sandside. The track would only have been readily accessible at low tide. The higher tides would have swept in here up to and beyond the present Sandside Road and almost up to 'Saltcotes Hall'.

The River Kent Front

The path, to the river side of the little shrubbery garden and the 1998 sea-defence wall, affords a view of the railway viaduct. The Kent viaduct, and the similar Leven viaduct a few miles to the west, made possible the connection of the Furness Railway, at Ulverston, to the Lancaster and Carlisle Railway at Carnforth. The Ulverston and Lancaster Railway was completed and opened on July 10th, 1857, the viaducts having taken less than a year to build. Initially constructed for single-track working they were modified for double tracks in 1862 when the Furness Railway Co. took over the whole system. As first constructed, and up to the time of the strengthening modifications made between 1915 and 1917, the viaduct virtually floated on the quicksands of the riverbed. The low hill, at the other end of the viaduct, is Meathop Fell.

The River Kent rail viaduct c. 1912

ARNSIDE RAILWAY VIADUCT

The Arnside viaduct is 522 yards (482 m.) long, a distance roughly equal to three times the height of Arnside Knott (159 m.), the hill rising up behind the village. The viaduct has 50 piers and hence 51 arches. The original viaduct was built on 50 sets of cylindrical iron piles driven down into the sand at the rate of two per tide, weather permitting. As no solid bottom could be found, even at a depth of 21.5 m., each pile was fitted with a circular plate foot. Compressed air, forced down the hollow pile, made it possible to drive the pile down to the required depth. At a depth of some 6 m., each of these plated piles was capable of supporting over 20 tons (around 20 tonnes). Thus each set of piles was capable of supporting well over 100 tons (about 100 tonnes). One of the spans is wider than the others being originally intended to allow ships to pass up to Sandside and Milnthorpe, as before. This short length of estuary shore was the only access to the sea that Westmorland had. The span was designed to be moveable sideways, as a drawbridge. Unfortunately, the estuary above the viaduct rapidly silted up and stopped the passage of trading vessels, negating the need for the retractable section. Although built initially as a single-track viaduct, it was designed so as to be easily converted to accommodate the double track by the addition of more piles. Before the railway, it had been possible to ford the river here at low tide. War, and the importance of the munitions' industry at Barrow, made it necessary to strengthen the viaduct. The piles were cased in concrete and brick. A limestone block and concrete apron was made across the base, apart from the main wide-span channel and a narrow channel against the Meathop shore. This 'curtain' wall, beneath the viaduct, effectively narrowed and deepened the river making safe crossing almost impossible except by boat. Early in the 20th century, the local doctor had to be ferried across to visit his Meathop and Witherslack patients.

In 1968 a new M6 to Barrow link road was proposed with creation of a second viaduct higher up the estuary. This in turn gave way to a possible Morecambe Bay Barrage that would have effectively sealed off the estuary from the sea. Both proposals were eventually turned down, following considerable local opposition, in 1972. The need for renewable energy sources has again raised the notion of a tidal lagoon feeding turbines through a barrage, such as at Cardiff.

The Promenade sea wall, in its original form, was constructed in 1897 but subsequently altered as the road was widened, The garden, here, was established originally as The Jubilee Garden to commemorate the Silver Jubilee of King George V. in 1935. Unfortunately the king died before the garden was completed in 1936 so, effectively, it commemorated the accession of King Edward VIII. Lady Stanley, wife of local M.P. Sir Oliver Stanley, officially opened the garden in September 1936.

The shore parking area, here, has been a bone of contention from early days of the 20th century. Many proposals have been made for enclosing the area with a sea wall to prevent the incursions of the water at the higher spring and storm tides. This would have allowed provision of a safe play area for children and a secure parking area.

Parking on the Foreshore 1969

Unfortunately the project has always proved too costly for the changing progression of responsible authorities. As an unofficial parking area, it was hoped, in 1964, that an honesty box might provide a little income. Within a month the box had been stolen! For a number of years thereafter an attendant was employed, from Easter to Autumn, to charge a parking fee on a 50/50 income basis. The system eventually collapsed when nobody was willing to take on the, sometimes, chilly job, even though a small shelter was provided. To partially counter flooding, a lot of spoil was spread over the area when a new sewer was being laid. More was added later as the result of gas installation. The large stones were introduced in the 1980s, on environmental protection grounds, to restrict the area of 'salt marsh' parked on by vehicles. Even this parking area can be flooded at the highest 'spring' tides or with adverse weather conditions.

Across the road, we look at the tall buildings on the other side. At the beginning of the 20th century the roadside sloped straight down to the shore. The road was then at a lower level and would frequently be flooded at the high tides. Until 1998, exceptional spring tides could flood the road, here, to a depth of 20 to 30 centimetres or more. (N.B. Variable height, spring tides occur every lunar month and not just seasonally.) Shopkeepers and house owners always kept sandbags at the ready. The new protection wall, built in the spring of 1998, minimised the problem. The houses, of which some now include shops, were built between 1890 and 1900. Originally, most of the block towards the right, with the archway, was Nelson's Temperance Hotel and Refreshment Rooms. Through the arch there were stables, now converted to a dwelling. Elijah Nelson was one of a number of Arnside entrepreneurs at the beginning of the 20th century. In addition to the hotel, he ran coaching and coal supply businesses and built Nelson's Victory Hall, in 1907. This, the first building on the left up Ashleigh Road, and now made into three houses, was an assembly hall and cinema for many years until at least the 1930s, and possibly longer. The coaching business was later to develop into a successful haulage firm, also based in Ashleigh Road, at the Trafalgar Garage. Until 2002 there was a large parking area for the garage vehicles, coaches and marine storage business. In 1928 his fleet of motor coaches included 'The Signal', 'The Flagship', 'The Trafalgar', 'The Victory', and 'The Nelson'.

In the 1920's, most of the estuary front properties provided accommodation. Visitors were well served by a number of grocers, eating places and refreshment rooms. A guidebook of the period indicates some 60 addresses offering accommodation in one form or another. At peak holiday periods the village population was said to almost double. A Carnforth Co-operative Society shop was established at the left hand end of Nelson's block before moving to larger, purpose-built premises, on the corner of Silverdale Road and Orchard Road, in 1909. The shop was then occupied, for many years, by Mr. Park a watch repairer and jeweller. Mary Pearson's charming gift shop, next to Ashleigh Road, was, successively, R.T. Pearson's Confectioners and Tea Shop; the premises of H. Walmsley, Plumber and Decorator; and a Fish and Chip shop.

Beyond Ashleigh Road the quaint pair of old cottages, facing the estuary, were early development properties built, around 1862, by the Barker family, then of 'Saltcotes', and providing visitor rooms. It has been suggested that they were occupied by two daughters of the family with a view to obtaining some 'pin money'. The census returns of the time would seem to indicate otherwise. Again, a touch of business acumen since, at that time, this would have been the nearest accommodation to the station, yet facing the estuary. It would have been 'one in the eye' for The Fighting Cocks inn, a few metres further on, as it was yet undeveloped to provide visitor accommodation as The Crown Hotel.

Ye Olde Fighting Cocks only assumed this name about 1970. About 1875, the lower portion, then The Fighting Cocks, had the taller, left-hand, section added. The new building assumed the name of The Crown Hotel, to accommodate visitors in the 'health' resort of Arnside. The lower part, which locally retained its original name, reputedly goes back to the beginning of the 17th Century as a riverside cottage and is, almost certainly, the oldest building on Arnside's estuary frontage. With the increase in estuary shipping, the cottage became an inn, about 1660. It is said that a cockpit existed in, or under, this building in earlier times but all evidence must now have been destroyed by modern redevelopment. An investigative 'dig' in 1974 failed to turn up any such evidence. Around the start of the 20th century, the village barber, Charles Bosworth, occupied a room to the right with an entrance up a flight of steps. About 1910 these steps were removed and the door replaced by a small window. In 2001 the steps and door were reinstated to provide an entrance to the renovated Lounge Bar.

The Crown Hotel c. 1910

It was probably close to here where George Fox held his Quaker meetings, in the middle of the 17th Century. He would have crossed the sands of the Leven Estuary and the Kent Estuary, by the fordable, guided routes similar to those now used by the cross-bay walkers, from that part of Lancashire, which, then, lay on the other side of the River Kent. The guides to the sands were appointed by royal warrant at least as far back as the reign of Henry VIII. The only safe access to the shore in Arnside would probably have been down the present Silverdale road by tracks from the south and west. People would have walked and ridden in from Beetham, Silverdale, the Yealands and possibly even further afield. The nearest Quaker Meeting House is to be found at Yealand Conyers a small village to the south on the original turnpike road.

A little further along, below the footpath, are a modern shelter and a toilet for the disabled. Currently, the Parish Council has ideas to turn the shelter end of the block into an ice-cream kiosk because of continued vandalism. It remains to be seen whether such a project could fare any better. The shelter replaced another of Victorian times, moved here in about 1929, with the help of The Arnside Advancement Association, from a shoreline quarry site further along the coast to the west. This Advancement Association was formed by village residents and shopkeepers, in 1927, to promote Arnside as a healthy holiday resort. It survived as an active group until the war curtailed its efforts in the 1940s. For many years, down in the corner to the left of the steps, was to be seen the original pump trough from which, until about 1890, many residents used to draw their water. Its original site was at a spring on the corner of Silverdale Road and Church Hill. The trough has now been resited, as a flower trough, in the middle of this, the Lower Promenade.

This Lower Promenade is the spot where the Customs House, and associated warehouses, stood until 1925. Until the cessation of the coastal shipping trade, with the coming of the railway in the 1850s, the customs' building was occupied by the Inland Revenue Coast Waiter. This officer would have controlled the revenue taxation regime for the estuary port of Milnthorpe, higher up the River Kent. Some of the associated buildings, on the site, would probably have been the equivalent of bonded warehouses holding liquor and tobacco. As the shipping trade had practically disappeared by 1860, the Customs' system no longer operated here. The buildings were taken over, and others added across the road, by the Bush family of The Albion Hotel, as storage and accommodation for their repository, haulage and horse-coach services. When William Bush died, in 1924, all the properties were sold at auction. Most of the buildings here were acquired by the, then, Westmorland County Council and were pulled down so that the road could be widened. The base of some of the original buildings was used to form this small leisure area. One warehouse, now the Sailing Club, still stands across the road, opposite the pillar clock erected in 1950, by former school pupils, in memory of the Bamford Family. The Bamfords were very much responsible for the success of Oakfield School, a private school for girls. This opened in 1884, and operated successfully in Arnside for nearly 70 years before moving to larger premises near Kirkby Lonsdale. The amalgamated school still exists in the Wokingham area as Luckley-Oakfield School.

The cottage lying up behind the Sailing Club building is 'Woodbine Cottage', one of the many homes of the Crossfield families, in Arnside, in the 19th Century. It had a commanding position, having been built by Thomas Crossfield, for his own occupation, probably about 1849 although it does not appear on early maps.

From here, beyond the trees alongside the sea-wall, we begin to see, more clearly, the compensation wharf, or 'pier', built by the railway company in 1865 to replace an older, probably rotten, wooden quay. It is said that the stone for the construction of Blackpool Promenade was brought from Sandside Quarry and loaded for boat transport here. Stout though it may look, it has, on a number of occasions, been partly reduced to rubble. Plaques, at the entry to the Pier, record that this last occurred as recently as 1983. It was rebuilt in 1984 but, owned by the Parish Council, resort had to be made to public donations to raise the money.

From the pier, the buildings along the front are seen, now, to be mainly shops. Here, the Victorian development of Arnside as a village and resort, rather than a mere hamlet, began.

About 1818, the Crossfields, father, John, and two sons, Thomas and Francis John, established a lath cleaving, and possibly barrel-making, business on the site of the old bank building at the left (with the lion crest over the door). Laths would have been used in building and fence making. The wood would have been obtained by coppicing on The Knott. Apart from a cottage and attached barn or workshop on this spot, there were no other buildings between The Fighting Cocks to the left and The Albion, at that time a private house, on the corner to the right. This cottage/workshop,

Centre Front c. 1903

some 35 metres long by 9 metres wide and lying at an angle to the shore track, was to develop into a building and boat building business from around 1838. It should be remembered that, prior to 1898, the shore sloped straight down to the water so launching a small boat would present little problem. The boat-building workshop and cottage were occupied by Francis J. Crossfield (Senior) and his family, until around 1880, when the business moved to Church Hill. There would only have been a cart track along the front to service The Fighting Cocks. It is suggested that some boat building took place in Arnside in the early 1700s but, so far, I have not found any firm evidence to support this idea. There is mention of a sloop 'The Leighton' but it is more likely that this was a cargo vessel bringing ore to the furnace at Leighton Beck, possibly repaired here but built elsewhere. Early maps also show this to be the original post office in Arnside. Following the move this first boatyard building was occupied by a Richard Booth as a smallholding. He was also a postman for the Post Office, which had moved to James Crossfield's shop. The building was to be demolished and replaced by a bank in 1895.

THE CENTRE FRONT SHOPS

Across the road from the Pier, we have the main shopping parade. Of this parade, only the Spar shop, the old District/NatWest Bank, Barclays Bank and probably Bay View, were purpose built commercial premises; the Spar (as Crossfield's) in 1863; Barclays (as The Bank of Liverpool, later Martins Bank) about 1880; the old NatWest (as The Lancaster Banking Co. later The District Bank) in 1895. The buildings, between

Post Office, West View and Marine View c. 1903

the Spar and the bakery, were built between 1860 and 1870 to house the increasing number of Crossfield families. The Spar was originally James Crossfield's Grocery Store and must have remained the only shop in the village until at least the 1880s when two small shops; another grocer's and a butcher's; were opened under the, then, Educational Institute in Pier Lane. The original Crossfield store incorporated the Post Office, probably soon after it opened but, by 1904, this had moved to the 'Little Shop', next door. This resulted when the premises were acquired, as a part of 'West View', and converted to a stationery shop by James Wilson. At this time Crossfield's had a glass verandah similar to those, which remain elsewhere. The shop remained a family business, as Crossfield's Grocers, for well over a hundred years. It is interesting to note that, even in 1903, there were two post collections and two deliveries each day, except Sunday. The Arnside station telegraph office, from where stamps could also be obtained, was open from 8 a.m. to 8 p.m.

There seems to be some evidence to indicate that 'Bay View' (the Café/Bakery) was altered in the 1890s. Plans show that it was originally built along the same line as adjacent 'Marine View' (the present chemist's) and later extended forward to form a new shop. It certainly left no room for a pavement at the time. The 1881 census shows it to have been occupied by a boot maker but this could have been just as a workshop. By 1891 it was the home of the local postman, Robert Thompson and his wife, and three children together with step-daughter, Sarah Walker. At the time of the census a family of five were also boarding in the premises. Thus there were 10 adults and one young child living 'behind' the shop.

About 1888 Frank Crosland, a London apothecary, married Mary Crossfield. Initially they were to live with her parents at 'West View'. Families were large and such households must have been very crowded. Again the census indicates that an extended 'West View' (The 'Country Shop') housed 3 families - 6 adults and 3 children in all. It seems likely that, about 1898, it was the Croslands who took over 'Bay View' and enlarged it to provide a proper pharmacy and darkroom space for his photographic work.

In 1903, 'Arnside House' was converted to Askews' Grocery Stores. Herbert Askew's wife was a Crossfield. One can only assume that the competition from James Crossfield's shop was too great, for the Askew shop was divided, by 1904, to accommodate Inchboards', Drapers and Milliners. By 1929 Askews' had partly changed direction for it now offered itself as a sweetshop, tobacconist, postcard and gift shop. Later conversions were 'Marine View', the present chemists and a pharmacy for many years, and 'West View' (the 'Country Shop' outfitters).

The 'Country Shop' was originally established, around 1908, as James Wilson's stationery and newsagents shop, together with post office. It had transferred from the small shop next to Crossfield's (now the Little Shop). Even with a forward extension covering about half of the present pavement the smaller shop was, presumably, not large enough. Wilson and his near neighbour, Frank Crosland, are important witnesses to Arnside history for they were both professional photographers and publishers of picture postcards. They seem to have exchanged photographic negatives from time to time. We remain indebted to them, and others, for many photographs of early Arnside.

25

James Wilson's stationery shop and Post Office in 1912

It would appear that, about 1904, Crosland decided to concentrate on his photography and card publishing business. Picture postcards were still somewhat of a novelty at this time and, presumably, provided a lucrative trade. The pharmacy business was taken over by Bamford, Taylor & Co. and moved next door into part of the newly converted 'Marine View'. This business was later to be taken over by F. Harrison, M.P.S. and eventually enlarged into something like its present form. The other, original, part of the conversion was opened as a Milliners and Ladies Outfitters, run by Mr. Oldham and Miss Gudgeon.

Later, when Wilsons at 'West View', had moved to 'Kentholme' next to Martins Bank, and Oldham & Gudgeon's next door, had closed, Timbrells' were established here as a ladies and gentlemen's outfitters. The shop door stayed in the middle, as originally converted. Around the 1960s the shop was taken over, firstly by the Cloughs and then by the Birrs, who renamed it as 'The Country Shop'. At some stage, the central door moved to the end and the through, open, side passage was blocked up. The Little Gift Shop, next to the 'Country Shop' and originally an infill extension to 'West View', was probably converted to a ground floor, lock-up shop for James Wilson, about 1903. In 1908 it was established as a shop (known as 'Leicester House') for Hammersley's, a boot and shoe business. This was soon to be taken over by Leightons, Boot and Shoe Makers, originally of Rock Terrace, behind the shops. The latter business endured for many years, having finally moved to 'Deaston House' presently Simon's Hairdressers, before closing in January 1956. Meanwhile, in all this movement and change, Crosland's shop at 'Bay View' was taken over by Caisleys, Cabinet Makers and Furnishers. This was to become W.A. Pearson's Ice Cream Saloon and, yet later, a bakery and café, as now.

The Wilsons moved along to the shop beyond the arch, next to the old Barclays' Bank (previously Martin's Bank and now estate agents, Ratcliffe & Bibby) in the 1920s. James was to concentrate on his photography and postcard business while his wife, Lizzie, acted as post-mistress and organised the 'emporium' side of the business. Eventually son, John, took over as post-master, and his sister, Ada, ran the general business side, apparently noted for being able to supply almost anything in the household line. The Post Office section was in the large window, with the stationery and general goods taking up the rest of the shop. John Wilson moved the Post Office into part of 'Deaston House' sometime after the war, only retiring to North Wales in the 1970s. Apparently no photographer, John merely reissued some of his father's cards. The other shop was taken over by Myers as a stationery and gift shop. In the 1980s it changed hands again to become a branch of Tarragon, a gift shop of Cartmel. Temporarily a branch of Lindale Textiles in the 1990s it became (in 1999) yet another move for the peripatetic Post Office.

Crossfield's store had been the only shop development here until about 1880. Apart from the old Barclays Bank, the taller properties were all developed as private houses from about this time. 'Deaston House' and 'Kentholme' were occupied by teachers but, no doubt, as the houses were large, they offered holiday accommodation. Simon, the present hairdresser's and next-door 'Photogenic', were to remain as houses until about 1910. 'Arnside House' was an early conversion to form Askews' Grocers. Later divided into two shops it was recombined in 2001, by the Smiths, as an enlarged 'Arnside House Gift Shop'.

'Tankerfield', where the butcher and greengrocer now ply their trades, saw the beginnings of two of Arnside's numerous private schools before inevitable conversion. Mrs. Proctor established the Ladies' Wesleyan Boarding School for Girls in 1884 and James Barnes started Arnside Boarding School for Boys in 1900. Both schools proved to be so successful that they had to move to larger premises elsewhere in the village. The house was originally called 'Earnseat' (an old spelling of Arnside) but when the boys' school moved to 'Inglewood', on the West Promenade, the name went with it. The girls' school moved to 'Oakfield', on Redhills Road, in 1895. 'Tankerfield' was to be another Crossfield residence, the name being derived from that of Mrs. Emily Tankard Crossfield. The ground floor of the original house was converted to shops about 1906. To start these were Wilkinson's, a fish, poultry and fruit shop, and Clarks, first butchers on the front. Later, Wilkinsons was to become Blyths, and in the 1980s and '90s, Lewthwaites greengrocers but in 2000 it was all change again. By 1907, a William Pearson had opened another greengrocery shop, underneath the Educational Institute, in Pier Lane.

On the shore, just beyond the Pier, are the stumps of an old wooden jetty, used by visitors to board the small boats, which plied for 'trips around the bay' from about 1870. It fell into disrepair about 1908 but the stumps have weathered the tides ever since.

Earnseat boys at 'Earnseat' (now Tankerfield) in 1902

The building across the corner, at the end of the shops, now 'The Albion Hotel', was originally 'Greenwood House', built about 1810, and home of mariner and coastal trading ship owner, Captain Robert Greenwood. Richard Bush, son of Captain Greenwood's maritime business partner, Ronald Bush, and himself a mariner, married Greenwood's daughter, Isabella. When Captain Greenwood died, in 1854, the house passed to Isabella and Richard. The impending construction of the new railway sounded the death knell of coastal shipping trade in the Kent Estuary. Richard altered the house and opened it up as 'Bush's Albion Hotel', complete with bars and function rooms. Later, Bush-family publicans were also to operate a coach and carriage business with stabling in Church Hill, just up beyond the hotel. Originally a smaller, plain fronted Georgian building, the house had two major extensions in the late 19th century and a variety of 'face-lifts' in the 20th. The gull-like piece of rock, mounted on the chimney, has been there for at least a century as has the large bell that can be seen on the back of the roof. The bell was probably used to summon the carriages in bad weather but may also have given warning as to the state of the tides, just as the bore siren does now.

The bore is a small tidal wave that fronts every incoming tide. It forms as a result of the narrowing funnel-shape of the estuary. The wave can be as much as a metre high but, normally, is only seen to be about half this height. The wave travels faster

The River Kent Bore in 1907

than you can run and with great force. The bare sands are covered in a matter of minutes to considerable depth. The rise and fall of the tide here vary between some 7 and 10 metres (more than the height of the average house), according to the time of year, the phases of the moon and weather conditions.

Silverdale Road runs up by 'The Albion'. This would have been the main track down to the estuary from Silverdale and the turnpike road to Leighton Beck, as the 'sands' route to the east would often be inundated by the tides. Up the hill were bridleways leading off to 'Saltcotes', New Barns, Arnside Tower and Far Arnside. The first road on the left is Church Hill. The house on the lower corner is 'Kent View Villa', built, in 1865, by Sam Wood, on his marriage to Isabella Crossfield, a sister of John Crossfield. She, too, came from Ulverston and would be the aunt of Thomas and Francis who were, by then, well established in the village. Although a cabinet maker by trade, Sam seems to have helped Richard Bush as a coal merchant. He may have had some connection with Caisleys, the cabinetmakers at 'Bay View'.

Church Hill, Church and Chapel

In the 18th century most of the land here was part of a farm, probably 'Wood Close Farm' belonging to a Thomas Saul but sold on to Ralph Bouskill in 1784. This land in turn passed to son Robert Bouskill of Hazelslack Tower Farm and then to the latter's brother John, a cordwainer (leatherworker) of Silverdale. The Bouskill farming families remained at Hazelslack so it seems likely that there was a wish to reduce their Arnside properties and take advantage of the increasing interest in land acquisition of potential, wealthy incomers to this hamlet. Part was sold to solicitor Stephen Simpson in 1802 for development of 'Wood Close House', possibly incorporating part of the farm. Other parcels of land would have been sold off from time to time. Thus Captain Greenwood would have built 'Greenwood House' and the Crossfields would have developed on the Front and later, Church Road. As the acreage of the property

Bush's Albion Hotel c. 1908

diminished so it passed down the generations finally, in 1855, to brothers Robert and John Bouskill. Their interests in Arnside finally disappeared as part of the land was sold to the Rev. William Hutton for the building of St. James' Church. Part was sold to a John Holme of Milnthorpe in 1870 and was to be developed by the Crossfields in the 1880s. Other parts were sold to Mr. Whitwell and to Mr. Barker of 'Saltcotes' eventually to become Orchard Road and adjacent properties.

Until the 1920s, Church Hill was called Church Road. Nobody seems to know who changed the name, or why! A short way up, on the left, is the entry to Rock Terrace. The workshops on the corner are those to which the Crossfields moved their building and boat-building businesses, probably in the 1860s. The delightful-looking little houses in the terrace, were, in the 1880s almost all homes for various branches of the Crossfield family. Beyond the workshops, still mainly occupied by Les Earl's carpentry, joinery and undertaking business, is 'Fern Bank', built for James (Grocer) Crossfield and backing on to his shop. The shop included a bakery extension for many years. 'Fern Bank', itself, has had an extension added at the lower end, now a separate dwelling.

Rock Terrace cottages

THE CROSSFIELDS OF ARNSIDE

There can be little doubt that the Crossfield families played a key role in the development of the village during the reign of Queen Victoria. The first Crossfields in Arnside were John and Margaret, married in Lancaster in 1805 but originally living with her parents, on their farm, at Arrad Foot, Ulverston. Two sons and four daughters were born to the couple between 1805 and 1816 though one daughter died in infancy in 1814. The eldest daughter, Margaret, was to marry Jonathen Titterington, publican at the Ship Inn, Sandside and, later, publican at The Crown and Fighting Cocks. The two sons, Thomas and Francis John, may probably be regarded as the most important members of the family. Evidence indicates that, about 1818, the whole family moved to Milnthorpe where John probably continued to work as a ship's carpenter, and possibly cooper, doing repair work for the coastal craft visiting the port. Both sons were apprenticed in the carpentry trades and were later able to join their father in a lath-cleaving business he created in Arnside about 1830. The family seems to have moved to 'Sea View', Silverdale Road, at this time. The business was established, close to the shore, in a shed on a site later (1895) to be occupied by a Lancaster Banking Co. Bank, which closed its doors, as a NatWest Bank, a century later, in 1996. The laths would have been used in house building and barrel making, in the first instance, but the same skills were,

from about 1838, to be applied to small boat building. The business, in its several facets, thrived with Thomas concentrating on house-building carpentry and Francis developing the boat building.

In the course of time Thomas and Margaret Crossfield had two sons, James and another Francis John. Margaret had opened a grocery shop at 'Sea View' in about 1845 and by 1855 was being helped by James. The family moved to 'Woodbine Cottage' in 1849. In 1863, James was to establish a new grocery shop on the estuary front called, simply, 'James Crossfield's'. He married Anne Gibson, of Arnside Tower Farm, the same year, and moved into a new house, behind the shop, in Church Hill. This was 'Fern Bank', to be a family home for many years. The Crossfield grocery business was to thrive for over a century before being sold on. It still exists as the Arnside 'Spar'.

Francis, the elder son, continued with his father as a joiner and carpenter and married Margaret Gibson, another daughter of Robert Gibson of Arnside Tower Farm, in 1864. They were eventually to move away to Barrow where the family established, and sustained, a thriving business as timber merchants. Last of this line of the family, in Arnside, was Robert Sands Crossfield, of 'Brantfell' in Redhills Road, who died in 1978. He had been successively a Parish, District and County Councillor in the 1950s and 60s. His widow, Mrs. Miriam Crossfield who died in 2001, was instrumental in creating the Abbeyfield Home at 'Brantfell'. It was to be named 'Crossfield House' in her husband's memory.

Meanwhile Thomas Crossfield's younger brother, Francis John, continued to develop the boat-building side of the business. Marrying in 1842, and again in 1853 after the death of his first wife, he was to father nine children of whom eight survived to adulthood. Many of the 5 surviving sons were to produce sizeable families of their own. Half-brothers, William and George, were largely responsible for carrying the business forward into the 20th century. The workshops had moved to Church Road around 1860 but as the family involvement increased so it was necessary to open an additional yard on the foreshore near Ashmeadow. This latter was to be developed, as the most successful of the businesses, by William Crossfield and his family. A letter heading of 1898 describes the business as "Joiners, Undertakers, Builders, Yacht and Boat Builders". Father, Francis John, had retired by this time to become the village Postmaster. The family businesses were to be responsible for the building of many houses and the production of hundreds of sailing vessels over a period of about a hundred and twenty years. The boats ranged from rowing boats to more ambitious vessels such as shrimpers, prawners and yachts, with even a few steam vessels in the 20th century. The Crossfield Brothers were responsible for many Arnside houses in the Victorian and Edwardian period. The firm would be responsible for the drawing up and submission of the plans and for the subsequent carpentry and joinery work. Houses on Church Hill and Mount Pleasant resulted from the family collaboration at this period.

The Church Hill business declined following the untimely death of George Crossfield in 1909. Around this time, several members of the family moved to Conway in North Wales and established yet another thriving boat-building business.

The Arnside workshops were sold on, around the start of the First World War, as a carpentry, joinery and undertaking business, which is what it remains to the present day. William Crossfield's sons, Fred and Francis, were to carry on the boatbuilding business, at the foreshore yard, until final retirement about 1951.

Now, at the beginning of the 21st century, only one surviving Crossfield resides in Arnside though, no doubt, there must be others related by marriage.

Opposite 'Fern Bank' is The Arnside Educational Institute. This building, extensively refurbished in recent years, was originally the new stables and coach-house blocks for 'Bush's Albion Hotel', dating from around 1880. At a later stage, an upper storey was added with function and meeting rooms, ladies' room, library and billiard room and an arched entry to the yard. It was used as an indoor camp centre by scout groups, boys' brigades and the like. It is still possible to make out the outlines of the arch through which the coaches and horses would pass although a glassed entry porch has been added in recent years. Stabling was also offered here for travellers' horses. Bush had originally acquired the Customs House and associated warehouses, on the shore-side, to establish a carriage and storage business. Establishment of the Church Hill premises allowed for considerable expansion. The last of the Bush family publicans at 'The Albion', William, died in 1923. The Church Hill buildings were sold for £1,000, at auction in 1924, to the Educational Institute, then in Pier Lane, as providing much larger premises and greater potential for expansion. The premises currently provide the community with a variety of facilities. The result is another prime example of voluntary action and co-operation in the village. The Institute was fortunate to benefit from a substantial legacy, in the will of Miss Nicholson, at the beginning of 2000. Miss Nicholson, one-time proprietor of The Inglemere Hotel (of which, more later), was an extremely talented lady who had been much involved with the social activities of the Institute, in particular its Drama section, an interest, which was to continue following her retirement from 'The Inglemere'. Some of this money enabled the provision of the slightly controversial, but sorely needed, car park across the road a little higher up.

ARNSIDE EDUCATIONAL INSTITUTE

When the fee-paying British School, originally on Briery Bank and now known as 'The Cottage', was forced to close around 1886, an exchange of premises was negotiated with the Crossfields such that the Pier Lane building could be acquired for a transfer fee of around £70. The newspaper reading room, library and meeting rooms, initially established in the school, were now transferred here as an independent institute. The meeting room was used largely for adult classes, both day and evening, and subjects included woodwork, needlework, art and cookery. There would appear to have been at least 80 paid-up members around the turn of the century. Thus the building became successively meeting room, Educational Institute, Roman Catholic Chapel and, eventually in 1978, Public Library though it had probably been built as a store for James Crossfield's shop. Various early shops and businesses; including William Pearson's Fruit and Vegetable shop, and

E. Moulding's barbers and hairdressers; were established in the lower middle half of the building, now largely occupied by a Building Consultancy firm and a café-restaurant, 'Café J'. The barbers, up the steps in the middle, closed in the 1980s. Originating, from around 1890, the shop rents were to boost the funds of the Institute.

The Institute was to move to its new premises in 1926 but shortage of ready finance, despite the sale of the Pier Lane premises, meant that some years were to elapse before it could be completely refurbished for its new role. Nevertheless the Institute's new premises were officially opened on September 16th, 1926 by Mrs. L. Gardner Thomson, wife of the, then, Chairman of the Parish Council. Change, preservation, development and improvement have continued ever since as enthusiasm and finance have become available. It is now, more than ever, a great asset to the village with a wide variety of facilities. These include a function and games hall with stage, billiards and snooker room; coffee bar and two meeting rooms that together can form a function suite; and finally another smaller meeting room. It now also provides the stage facilities for The Arnside Players following a move from the Women's Institute Hall some years ago. The whole is complemented by a small bric-a-brac shop that provides a significant contribution to E.I. finances and grant aid to other village interests.

The Parish Council Office has been situated in part of the ground floor for a number of years. The room, in earlier days, was used by a Miss Lishman as a small, infants' school.

The Parish Council came into being in the spring of 1897 when the population of Arnside outgrew the rest of the Parish of Beetham. Parish councils had been established in 1893 and Arnside, as a part of the civil Parish of Beetham had, until 1897, been in the control of Beetham Parish Council, established in 1894. The latter had had several elected members from Arnside who, in the event were elected to the new Arnside Council. Thus the new council took over some of the concerns of The Ratepayers and Property Owners Association which had been formed in 1888 because of the poor state of the roads, the lack of any street lighting, flooding, and the poor postal and train services. One outcome was the employment of a council contractor to attend to such things as minor repairs to roads, paths and walls; street sweeping and litter collection. It is recorded that in the 1940s the contractor, probably Thomas Willacy, combined the tasks of roadman, scavenger, footpath maintenance man, sexton, cemetery caretaker and gravedigger. Latterly, Council maintenance work and grave digging have been in the hands of Reg. Taylor and family. In the 1990s, Tony Spedding, a local character, did cheery and efficient service as road sweeper, bin emptier and warning siren operator.

Originally with 7 members and now with 11, the Parish Council, for over a century, has tried to serve the best interests of the electorate though, latterly, few elections have been held. With an electorate around 2,000 it is sad to find that so few are willing to give some time and effort to this important aspect of service to the community. I write as a retired Parish Councillor, and one time Vice-Chairman, serving for a period of 11 years. More of the Council's history can be gleaned from my centenary monograph, 'Arnside Parish Council - 1897 to 1997 - A Centenary of Community Service'. Mention should be made of the longest serving Chairman, Vic Gray MBE now retired, who continues to do sterling work in the community. Thanks must also be extended to the several Clerks to the Council, one of whom, Walter Chorley, served, in that office, for 43 years. Mrs. Marian Ball, Clerk since 1983, retired only in 2002. Councillor David Willacy, a native of Arnside, does yeoman service on the present council.

Next above the Institute, is 'Greenwood House'. This was built in 1900 by Richard Bush, probably in retirement, for his wife Isabella (Greenwood), daughter of Captain Greenwood of the original 'Greenwood House', now The Albion. They did not stay long as a school opened there in 1902. This was to be another private school for boys, founded by the Owner, H.H. Llewellyn, J.P. It soon flourished and moved, in 1904, to larger premises on High Knott Road, as Aylwin College. An associate girls' school was to be founded at 'Inglemere House' in 1905.

Opposite, we find Pier Lane, leading down to the Promenade. 'Carr Garth', on the corner, was the business premises of W.E. Ward, Plumber, Painter and Decorator in the 1920s before moving down to the Promenade. Down Pier Lane, on the left, is yet another Crossfield building, presumably a store, or even the bakery, for James Crossfield's shop. It was probably used as a Wesleyan Methodist meeting room, around 1874, following the death of Robert Gibson at Arnside Tower Farm. In 1886 it was acquired as the Educational Institute following the demise of the 'British' School on Briery Bank. When the Institute moved in 1926 the building was acquired as a chapel of ease by the Catholic Church and named 'Our Lady of Lourdes'. Presently, and since 1978, it houses the local County Library, in its upper level,

Robert Gibson, *Yeoman Farmer and Methodist Preacher*

Robert Gibson, a farmer born in Langdale in 1797 and raised in Kendal, took over Arnside Tower Farm in 1832. He soon started to hold prayer meetings in his home, at the farm. Among the congregation, in later years, were two sons of carpenter Thomas Crossfield, James and Francis John Crossfield. Eventually the two young men married two daughters of Robert Gibson. It would be interesting to know whether the initial attraction lay with Wesleyan Methodism or with the young ladies. Suffice to say that the young men were soon hooked on both counts. When Robert Gibson died in 1873, James Crossfield, by then owner of the only shop in Arnside, made provision for meetings to be held firstly, in his home at 'Fern Bank', and then, almost certainly, in the Pier Lane premises practically next door. The Chapel, opened a few years later, was dedicated as The Robert Gibson Memorial Chapel. Robert Gibson and his wife are buried in Silverdale.

Continuing up Church Hill we see, on the right, a row of tall, Victorian semi-detached and terraced houses 'built' by the Crossfields between 1880 and 1900. The earlier houses, here, were provided with basement cisterns, connected to the roof gutters, to save walking down to the pump at the bottom of the hill. An adequate mains water supply only arrived in 1906 when water was piped from Lupton to a header tank opposite the cemetery. (The inspector for the scheme was an Augustus H. Strongitharm!) The water had previously been piped across the estuary from Grange having originated from tarns above Cartmel but the pipes were often damaged by exceptional tides. Initially, several of the houses were occupied by the more wealthy Crossfields. As business declined and families moved away so the houses passed on to others. In 1937, the Misses Fairbank established a boarding school for girls, ages 4 to 14, at 'Hare Hill'. The girls wore smart blue uniforms. The 40-bed Y.H.A. was opened at 'Broadlands' here, in 1946, but moved to Redhills Road in 1971. Ben Myers was hostel warden for a long period from 1952. On the left, 'Oakroyd', the house by the lane down to 'Woodbine Cottage' and the Promenade, was completed about 1880 and occupied by a widow, Mrs. Marian Toulmin. The lane was known as Toulmin Lane, in her lifetime, but this was later corrupted to Toll Lane. It is suggested that the Crossfields exacted a toll for vehicular use of the lane. Even the use of this name has now lapsed. The houses in upper Church Hill date mainly from 1905. Exceptions are 'Sladen Mount' and 'Railway Cottages' (now 'Church View Cottages') down the station path. When built, in the 1870s, the cottages were occupied by rail employees, porters, platelayers and a signalman. Houses beyond the church date, mainly, from the 1930s.

The Parish Church, completed in 1866, lies near the summit of the hill, on the right, tucked in among the houses with the adjacent, modern, National School. When built, there would be no other buildings close to it. St. James' Parish Church would have

St. James' Church c. 1912

been quite isolated in 1866 and the parishioners relatively few. Access would have been by the track up where Church Hill now lies, and by the path running past it in both directions. The new church was consecrated by the Lord Bishop of Carlisle on 5th July 1866. First baptism at the font was that of John Edgar, son of George and Jane Edgar of Black Dyke Farm. The first Vicar, William Kivell Stevens, was to serve the parish for some 27 years.

Although relatively plain, the interior is very pleasant. The colourful East Window, in memory of Thomas Rodick, local worthy and churchman who died in 1873, is well worth viewing as are the windows in the small memorial chapel to the war dead, next to the chancel. Other windows in the South Aisle commemorate individuals who died in the First World War. The Rodick window appears a little odd as it is attributed to Thomas Rodick of Ashmeadow. Though retaining ownership of Ashmeadow, he had lived in Beechwood House and then Wood Close, since 1849? The original church, built at a cost of £1,600, was basically the nave and choir of the present one.

At various times it has been extended by adding two extra bays to the length, plus North and South aisles. The extensions were prompted partly by the increasing population, around the turn of the century, and by the proliferation of private boarding schools between 1900 and 1910. During the Second World War the Vicar, the Reverend

Bank Holiday outing to the Fairy Steps in 1905

William Brailsford, was the Officer in Charge of the Milnthorpe based Home Guard. In the 1980s, with declining congregations, the arches of the North aisle were enclosed with wooden shutters effectively to provide a separate church meeting room.

Before 1866, Arnside lay in the parish of Beetham with its church about two and a half miles away by poor paths and tracks. The shortest path route involved negotiating the scarps of Whinscar, on Beetham Fell, by the aptly named, very narrow, Fairy Steps. As a coffin or 'corpse' route it was necessary to haul the coffins up the two scarps with ropes secured through ring bolts. The steps were too narrow to negotiate otherwise. It appears to have been a popular walking route for visitors.

The new, ecclesiastical, Parish of Arnside was created and defined, both on paper and by a series of boundary marker stones, in 1870. Traces of these latter can still be found; on Cold Well Lane at Creep-i'-th'-Call (originally Creepock Hole) bridge; on Dollywood Lane near Haverbrack; and on Cockshot Lane near Storth.

The Vicarage lies almost opposite the church on Church Hill at a house originally known as 'Shianmhor'. The former occupants, finding the house a little large in their retirement, had a new bungalow built in their orchard and moved the house name, and themselves, to it. The original vicarage was situated, about a kilometre away, up Silverdale Road. A peculiar choice of position considering that when built in 1871, almost in isolation, there were so few other buildings close to the church itself. A Sunday School, later the National School and now the Catholic Church, was built on Silverdale Road in 1880.

The modern Church (National) School lies on the South side of the church having moved here from Silverdale Road in the 1970s. Alongside the school is a small terrace of cottages, 'Wood Close Cottages', and a narrow public footpath, which is a section of one of Arnside's oldest rights of way. This narrow, walled path passing 'Felsteads', the old Junior School House of Inglemere School for Girls, leads out on to Orchard Road. On the opposite side of the road lies the Arnside Women's Institute and Village Hall. Orchard Road was originally two cul-de-sacs the upper portion then being Meadow Street, a name that is now only echoed in 'Meadowbank', the long terrace of houses. The large house above the Hall was built for the village doctor in the 1920s and then known as 'Hungersheath'. Later the practice, and eventually the house, were taken over by Dr. Alex Matchett and renamed 'Orchard Close'. With his wife Gwen, Dr. Matchett was to serve as Arnside G.P. for 44 years before retiring. He handed over to his son, Dr. Andrew Matchett who, also living in Orchard Road, was to develop the existing, flourishing group practice and medical centre.

The Women's Institute started in Arnside in 1919 and, largely by the efforts of its co-founder and then President, Mrs. Heath, was able, in 1928, to have this admirable hall built for the use of the whole community. During the Second World War, part of the main hall was divided up to provide small offices for various community service groups such as Civil Defence (an Air Raid Wardens Post), National Savings, and Welfare Services (milk powder and orange juice, etc.). It accommodated the village's First Aid Post during this period. Hooks remain in the ceiling to show where camouflage netting was made for the forces. In the 1950s the hall was used as the

1927 Architect's sketch of the new Women's Institute and Village Hall

village cinema with seats at 1/-, and 6d. for children. At other times, both before and after the war, it has been used for various play productions by the Dramatic Society and the Arnside Players. Still owned and run by the W.I., the hall provides yet another welcome venue for social events, lectures and coffee mornings, as well as W.I. meetings, throughout the year. It is presently home to two Institutes - Arnside and Arnside Knott. The former meets in afternoons while the latter meets in evenings thereby largely catering for those otherwise occupied with families or business during the day.

The narrow pathway, from the church, continues to the west of the W.I. Hall to emerge into Chapel Lane opposite the Wesleyan Methodist Chapel. The large semi-detached houses, next to the chapel, date from the beginning of the 20th century. The chapel was built, following the death of Robert Gibson in 1874, and dedicated as The Robert Gibson Memorial Chapel in his memory. The entrance is to the left and here, in the right-hand wall, can be seen all the various commemorative foundation stones, some dating back to the time of the original, 1875 building. The chapel was dedicated on June 30th 1876. Inside, we note the stained glass memorial windows and the refined simplicity of the decoration. Windows are dedicated to the Rev. J.M. Bamford, (the Bamford family were greatly involved with Oakfield School for Girls. 'Oakfield House' had been the family home); to James and Anne Crossfield, son-in-law and daughter of Robert Gibson; and a Peace Thanksgiving window. As in the case of St. James, it was found necessary to enlarge the chapel around the turn of the century. A new chapel nave was built at right angles to the original, simple, rectangular building and the latter then incorporated to form the two existing transepts. The schoolroom, across the back, had been added some ten years earlier. The Charles Garrett Memorial Organ was installed in 1903. The manse now lies next door to the chapel at 'Arnmore' but, from 1907 until the 1930s, was located at a house in Ashmeadow Road.

SILVERDALE ROAD AND TOP O' THE HILL

Chapel Lane leads out on to Arnside Hill and Silverdale Road. The cottage, on the right-hand corner, was a stable and coach house, most likely, for the, then, occupant of 'Arnmore'. Both buildings were certainly there in 1878 and I still consider that they may have been provided as the first manse since the Ashmeadow Road houses were not built until the 1890s. Much later, when stables were no longer required, it became Arnside's first Fire Station but is now an attractive private house. The Reverend Ash Parsons, Minister about 1912, visited his parishioners on a motorcycle!

Left, up the hill, is a pair of tall, semi-detached cottages - 'Anston Cottage' and 'Sea View'. These were probably built in the early part of the 19th century and the latter was, most likely, the first home of the Crossfields in Arnside. It is certainly suggested that their first grocery shop was opened here by John Crossfield's wife, Margaret, about 1845.

A few metres further up lies the entrance to 'High Bank' with its stout, stone gateposts. Across the road, to the right, are two similar gateposts adjacent to an obvious drive and gatehouse. This is the original entry to 'Ashmeadow', a large property

The Inglemere Hotel entrance on Silverdale Road

down on the sea front, of which more later. All were owned by a wealthy merchant, William Berry, who came to live there about 1816. 'High Bank' was the original coach-house and stables and was surmounted by a large bell-tower. The bell, together with a similar one at 'Ashmeadow' about a quarter of a mile away, was used to carry signals between the house and the coachmen when a coach was required down at the house. The lines of the old archway can still be discerned in the centre of the building, now converted into three dwellings.

    The next large building, 'Claremont', now apartments, was originally an accommodation block for Inglemere School for Girls, which was situated on the other side of Silverdale Road, here. Possibly for the convenience of visiting parents, part of the ground floor was given over to Miss Overend's Tea Rooms. Latterly it was owned by Miss Nicholson it having been effectively an annexe to the Inglemere Hotel of which she had been proprietor until retirement. The Hotel, now demolished, was replaced by the Inglemeres housing estate. An elephant, which had originally stood outside the door of the hotel, was for many years to be seen on Miss Nicholson's rooftop patio outside her penthouse flat at 'Claremont'. It was removed when the flat was put up for sale in 2001. The whole block had formed part of Miss Nicholson's legacy to the Educational Institute following her death in 2000.

    Higher still lie 'Rose Cottage', a tiny mews coach-house block, and 'Sunnycote'. All these buildings were associated with 'Springfield House' one of the older, early 19th century residences of the village, in Springfield, round the corner, and dwarfed

The Arnside branch of the Carnfoth Co-Operative Society, 1969

by its late 19th century additions. In 1849 it was known as 'Morecambe Cottage' and occupied by Thomas Rodick, (Junior). It would have then had fine views over the estuary. A few years earlier, in 1845, Rodick is listed as living in 'Hill Top House'. By its position it is probable that both these names refer to the same house. Earlier in the 20th century, 'Sunnycote' was an Art and Crafts Depot selling leather goods, silks, china and art materials. More recently it was a pet shop but reverted in 1996 to being a private dwelling. The modern developments in Springfield are relatively recent and occupy the area of the original large garden of 'Springfield House'.

The next block, often known as 'Top o' the Hill', includes a number of houses and shops dating from the first quarter of the 20th century. The grocer's at the corner of Orchard Road was, originally, a purpose-built shop for the Carnforth Co-op when it moved from its original position, in Nelson's building, in 1909. It opened with a great flourish on the 23rd of April that year with an opening ceremony on the following day, Saturday April 24th.

It is likely that all the other shops in this row, apart from the small premises tacked on the end, were originally private houses converted in the 1920s and 30s. Premises now occupied by Westworths' Electrical shop were, for many years, Oversbys' 'Dainty Café' and the associated grocery store. Alongside this was Holmes' Wools and Haberdashery shop though Miss Holmes was reputed to sell almost everything! This

Meadowbank Terrace, Orchard Road

latter reverted to being a private house in 1996 after a chequered life fostering various trades. The tiny single-storey shop, on the end, was occupied by Arthur Askew, footwear specialist and shoe repairer for almost 50 years, until his death in 1997.

Across the road was to be found Dodds 'Green Café' in what was later to be Birkett's Bakery and Café until 2000. It then became an extension of the Dental Surgery, next door. The surgery had also been a shop, handling a variety of trades, since the early 1900s.

Orchard Road was originally two separate parts divided by Mr. Whitwell's orchards. The upper part, started about 1890, was known as Meadowbank Road after a house, there, named 'Meadowbank' (now 'Glenroyd'). The long row of terraced houses was called Meadow Bank Terrace. Eventually, about 1920, the two parts were joined to form a through road.

Until the mid-1980s, the lower house of the semis opposite Chapel Lane was the village police station. With continued economies in policing the station was closed and responsibility moved to the Milnthorpe office.

Down the hill, below Chapel Lane, was 'Arndale Café'. Prior to this it had been 'Shepherds' Café' following a move from Station Road. The name Crossfield appeared, in mosaic tiling, in the entrance doorway. This property has reverted to being a private house, 'Arnside Hill', having been a café for a number of years. It had been just another example of Crossfield family enterprise in days gone by having been William Crossfield's haberdashery business. He was another son of William (Boat-builder) Crossfield. The new owners, having had the shop window and door filled in, have relocated the mosaic into the surface of their small forecourt which did not exist in the early part of the century. Next door lower down 'Springbank', also refurbished as a private dwelling, had previously been a Bric-a-Brac shop, now located next to the Sailing Club on The Promenade. At a considerably earlier date it was 'The Two of Clubs Café' and before that the Telephone Exchange.

In the 1920s, Miss Barwise supervised a Registered Nursing Home at a house in Ashmeadow Road. Here too, for many years in the earlier part of the 20th century, was the Methodist Church Manse.

Beyond the lower end of Orchard Road, are the two large gardens of 'Arncrag' and then 'Wood Close'. These were once all the land of 'Wood Close', built about 1802 for solicitor Stephen Simpson and, in the mid-nineteenth century, occupied by Robert Preston Rodick. Robert predeceased his father in 1859 when only 37. The house was apparently still owned by his father, Thomas Rodick, (Senior) who, in about 1842, had acquired a licence to hold religious services there. He was to be one of the main patrons and sponsors of the new St. James' Church. Rodick (Senior) had moved into 'Beechwood (Beachwood) House' in 1849 but apparently moved back to 'Wood Close' at some time in the 1860s. The window above the altar is to his memory. At one period around the 1960s the house was occupied by a Mr. & Mrs. Stark, licences of 'The Crown Hotel'. They ran a café on the ground floor of the property, at this time. The house changed hands but remained intact until 1992 when it was scheduled for conversion to several flats. In 1998 an additional four new houses were also added to create ten dwellings in all. The remaining piece of the original house is probably the oldest, purely residential, property in the village. Other old properties were inns or connected with agricultural and craft trades.

At the corner of Church Hill there is nearly always a trickle of water at the foot of the wall of 'Wood Close'. This is one of the few springs in Arnside and was the original site of the village pump. Although some mains water came to the village in the 1880's, the pump and trough were not removed until 1934. As previously mentioned, the trough still lies in the Lower Promenade area, and is now a flower tub.

On the opposite side of the road, the double fronted shop, originally 'Regent House', has again had a chequered existence. It would

Kent Villa and the old village pump c. 1920

appear to have been, amongst other things; Whittakers Fruit and Vegetable Shop; Williams Fruit and Vegetable Shop; Albert Wood's Electrical Shop; Kenneth Gardner's Radio and Television; an Art and Gift Shop; a Bric-a-Brac Shop and, currently (2002), a Sandwich Bar.

THE WEST PROMENADE AND BEACHWOOD BEACH

The West Promenade starts opposite 'The Albion Hotel'. The first block of houses, here, was also the last to be built, about 1904, replacing the large garden of next-door 'Grosvenor House', then the Misses Mackereths' 'Grosvenor Hotel'. In the 1930s there was a coach shelter here, alongside the garden wall, for this was a terminus for the Milnthorpe bus. The other houses along the front were built largely between 1883 and 1900, starting with the atypical 'Old Sandhurst', beyond 'Holly Bank'. Originally 'Sandhurst', it was completed in 1884, as the wall plaque over the door testifies. It seems a pity that an earlier owner would appear to have fallen on hard times and sold part of the land to permit intrusion of a modern dwelling to spoil the Victorian line. In the late 1930s, 'Sandhurst' was used as a small mental home. Although most houses were occupied by families, they were built so as to provide seasonal holiday accommodation on a bed and breakfast, or self-catering basis. There are few such premises in Arnside now, but in the 1920s some 50 or 60 holiday addresses were

Sandhurst, the first house built on the West Promenade in 1884

listed in the local guide. There were notable exceptions such as Earnseat School and 'Braeside', home of Electrical Engineer Thomas Wilkinson. Originally only 'Sandhurst' had the wide 'drive-in' gateway, which still exists, at an angle to the road. It can only be presumed that the original occupiers were wealthy enough to have a carriage, which was probably accommodated, in Bush's stables. Until after the Second World War, all the other houses had just small gates. The growth in car ownership altered that and more now have wide entrances.

There is an old drinking fountain on the other side of the road, here. At the beginning of the century, the local doctor, Dr. Grosvenor, lived in Grosvenor House, in the second block. The memorial fountain was erected in 1904, by the doctor's parents, in memory of their grandson, Richard, who, born on July 11th, 1899, died on June 22nd, 1903. Nearing his fourth birthday, he died from complications of appendicitis. A bronze relief of the face of Richard Mobberly Clayton Grosvenor appears on the front of the fountain. In a slightly sad state and refurbished a number of times, the fountain still stands as a prominent meeting point where Royal Proclamations are read as the occasion dictates. The Arnside Brass Band was present at the Proclamation for King Edward VIII in 1936. Up to 1961 there were two stepping-stones, either side of the trough, to enable children to reach the tap. They were thrown on to the foreshore by vandals and never replaced.

45

Cedric Robinson (centre) leads a Cross-Bay Walk in 1989

This West Promenade was the fashionable place to be seen when visiting this popular seaside resort in the first half of the 20th century. The beach here would be crowded with families playing games and picnicking or even listening to a band. Here, too, parents of children at the various boarding schools would stroll with their offspring prior to having tea at one of the several cafés in the village or at Beach Walk, near the boatyard. Nowadays the Promenade here sees the start of the many cross-bay walks, which take place in the summer season. Organised for many years by the Queen's Guide to the Sands, Cedric Robinson, the walk of six or seven miles and a few hours duration, eventually reaches dry land again at Kent's Bank, on the other side of the estuary. While many large crowds of people tackle the walks to raise money for charities, they do not always endear themselves to the village community by causing traffic and parking problems in a village hardly designed to cope with such an influx.

Further along were to be found 'Norwood', 'Merlewood' and 'Earnseat'. The latter, originally called 'Inglewood', was taken over by Mr. J.M. Barnes, in 1902, as larger premises for his 'Earnseat Boarding School for Boys'. This had been started at a house called 'Earnseat', in the central shopping parade, in 1900. The name moved with the school, which, henceforth, was to be known as 'Earnseat School for Boys'. It expanded again in 1918 with the acquisition of 'Ashmeadow', a large house at the end of the Promenade. Successful for some 70 years, 'Earnseat School' finally closed in 1971 but the name remains in the memory of many who had associations with it. Apart from 'Norwood', a private hotel, all the school's premises were leased and occupied by an adventure-training establishment, Lakeland Training, until about 1990 when the scheme went bankrupt. This occurred as the result of an unsuccessful venture, called 'Operation Innervator', a sub-unit of the New Directions Foundation, which used converted buses to bring adventure training to the inner cities and to make goodwill trips to run-down cities of Eastern Europe.

After this, a fallow period and the death of John Barnes, owner, son and successor to the founder, led to some of the still empty premises having to be sold off. In 1996/97 the original 'Earnseat' was resurrected as 'Herons Reach' containing a number of apartments. Similarly the semi-detached 'Norwood' and 'Merlewood' houses have been converted to form 'Inglewood Court'.

Operation Innervator bus, 1988

Earnseat during conversion in 1996

EARNSEAT BOARDING SCHOOL FOR BOYS

In 1900, James Barnes started a school for boys at 'Earnseat House', (now 'Tankerfield') in the middle of the present central row of shops. This was 'Arnside Boarding School for Boys'. Apart from Crossfield's Store and Crosland, the Apothecary, all the buildings along the front were private houses at this time. 'Earnseat House', home of a teacher, had seen the start of a girls' school in 1884. This school had been sold on as a going concern and moved to 'Oakfield' in 1895.

James Martindale Barnes, the founder of the boys' school, was assisted with certain aspects of the curriculum by brother, John Anthony Barnes, and their sister, Annie. The former was responsible for the first published, brief history of Arnside, 'All Around Arnside', in 1903.

The school would appear to have prospered and outgrown its premises very quickly for it was to move along to a large detached house, called 'Inglewood', on the new West Promenade. The 'Earnseat' name went with the school so 'Inglewood' became 'Earnseat' and remained as such until 1996. In 1905 the school expanded into, next door, 'Merlewood'.

J.M. Barnes, Head (seated), with staff and boys in 1904

The school continued to develop and progress, so much so that, in 1918, James Barnes was able to buy 'Ash Meadow' following the death of the previous owner, John Pyke Wilson. This mansion, at the end of the West Promenade, gave considerable scope for expansion as it not only more than doubled available rooms but provided several acres of open space and woodland for sporting, recreational, nature study and artistic activities. 'Earnseat' became a school boarding house as did 'Merlewood' one of the semi-detached houses next door. The other house, 'Norwood', a private hotel in the 1950s, was also later to be used by the school as the headmaster's residence with a Senior boys, common room in the basement. As already mentioned, these two houses have now been converted to flats as 'Inglewood Court'. Similarly, 'Earnseat' is now 'Herons Reach'.

A temporary, but tragic, set-back for the school, in July 1918, was the loss, by drowning in the estuary, of Senior Master, H.M. Ashley, and a pupil, E.R. Cardwell. This led to the construction of the swimming pool in the grounds of 'Ash Meadow'. Work started in May 1919, after money had been donated by the parents, and was to be completed, as an open seawater pool, by the autumn of that same year. It was dedicated as the 'Ashley and Cardwell Memorial Pool - 17.7.1918'. It was not to be until about 1970 that the pool was covered with a plastic roof and new heating and filtration plant installed. Previously the pool had used filtered water pumped in from the estuary and changed about twice a month. It is reported that "the water was somewhat brown and there were often small jellyfish swimming about"!

The extra space was to be put to good use in the ensuing years. The original walled kitchen garden continued to give produce, particularly during the years of the Second World War. The garden cottage, originally the estate gardener's dwelling, was, eventually, turned into an art room complex having, at one period, been used as an aviary. It is said that pupil Julian Heaton Cooper was partly responsible for the wall murals in this room. Unfortunately the damp has almost completely destroyed them. An open-air aviary also existed outside the eastern end of the walled garden. There was a hen-run and other livestock, such as rabbits and guinea pigs, were accommodated close by. It is recorded that, in the lifetime of the school, there had also been sheep, goats, hamsters, gerbils and a donkey. A wooden framed building, acquired from Mr. Llewellyn on closure of 'Aylwin College' on High Knott Road, was rebuilt up in the woods, close to the walled garden, to provide a sizeable gymnasium. Not a thing of beauty, being clad largely in black corrugated iron, it was, nevertheless, completely adequate for its multi-purpose usage. In later years a hard tennis court was constructed close to the gymnasium. This space, now in private hands, has recently been converted back to its original purpose.

The school catered for some 70 pupils with a wide curriculum and a basis of structured activity in environmental studies. The now scant remnants of the periodical, duplicated, school magazines indicate the wide range of academic and leisure pursuits together with literary and artistic talent. On the 4th February 1916 the boys were excited to see the steam yacht 'Mona Loa' anchored off the Promenade. This belonged to a Mr. Calvert of Fleetwood. It is recorded that, in 1959, the boys found a large anchor on the edge of the salt marsh above the viaduct. They constructed a raft of oil drums and managed to float it down to Ashmeadow.

James Barnes was eventually, in 1941, to be succeeded as headmaster by his son, John A.G. Barnes, who, having been a pupil at the school, had progressed to a Cambridge degree. He returned, around 1935, to become an assistant master on the school staff. On marrying, his wife Dorothy was to become a help to mother-in-law, Mrs. Celia Barnes, and thereby one of the mainstays of the domestic side of the school until John Barnes' retirement in December 1968.

In its heyday, Earnseat School had been able to board and educate between 60 and 70 boys with around 6 permanent staff and a number of part-time specialists. Particular attention was given to outdoor activities, the school having its own minibus transport, a dinghy and a number of canoes in its later days. Many pupils

Earnseat School cricket at Ashmeadow c. 1930

gained places at public schools, notably Sedbergh, progressed to university, and went on to be very successful civil servants, scientists, engineers, businessmen and army officers. As with many boarding schools a number of pupils had parents who, living in the colonies, desired an English school education for their sons.

Mention can be made of a few Old Boys who managed to achieve mentions in 'Who's Who?'. Note, in several cases, the Crossfield connection. - - -

Sir Walter Crossfield Hankinson, sometime High Commissioner for Ceylon.

Sir Thomas Robinson Ferens, Company Director in Hull.

Frederick Crossfield Happold, Headmaster and Author.

Robert Sands Crossfield, High Sheriff of Westmorland (1970-71).

In the 1966, 'Earnseat' became an Educational Trust school. With the retirement of Mr. Barnes, Mr. R. Cleveland took over as headmaster in January 1969. The school was finally closed, as a boarding school in 1979.

Further along is 'Braeside'. In 1900, this was the home of electrical engineer, Thomas Wilkinson. In 1903 he installed the first direct current electricity generator in Arnside in a building in Back Lane, behind the house. Having successfully brought electric light to his own house, he soon expanded the system to supply the nearby school, then other houses in the village and, eventually, even houses in Grange, across the estuary. The generator building still remains but the responsibility for power generation, and a change to alternating current, was eventually taken over by the Electricity Board. Wilkinson supplied all forms of lighting and electrical gear, including lighting for outdoor spectaculars, and introduced the first telephone to the village in 1905. He was an active member of the Parish Council and its Chairman, for a short period, in the 1920s.

A storm, in November 1977, caused severe damage to the sea wall along this part of the front and much chaos in the shore-quarry boat park. The damage was soon rectified but the opportunity was taken to increase the width of part of the road by about a metre and a half, a factor that was later to help with the echelon parking of the present time. Opportunity was also taken to provide the steel tube safety fencing along the top of the wall. It was at this time that there were proposals for the new dinghy and boat park later established in Grubbins Field.

ASHMEADOW HOUSE

At the end of the Promenade, stands the gated entrance to 'Ashmeadow' (but originally 'Ash Meadow'). This imposing Georgian mansion, dating from about 1816, was built around an old riverside inn. This had been converted to a dwelling about 1810 and sold on to wealthy businessman, William Berry, for under £70, in 1815. Berry had interests in the estuary shipping trade and owned a large warehouse, which still exists, at the back of Quarry Lane, Sandside. The estate had imposing gardens and a large orchard but, in the course of time and with change of use, these have virtually disappeared. The property was depicted in an etching published as part of an article in a Lonsdale Magazine of 1822. Substantially, the present main house remains just as it appeared so many years ago, despite several changes of occupancy. An obvious addition however, seen from the west end, is the hipped roof in the centre. Originally a low-ceilinged, flat-roofed room, it was to be converted in the 1930s, by the then school, to form a stage at the end of a large room at the front corner of the first floor.

A private house until 1918 and, now, a Grade II listed building, it became a further enlargement of Earnseat School on the death of the, then, resident recluse, John Pyke Wilson. During the school period, some 60 years, various changes were made to the grounds. In 1933 the boys created the, now almost hidden, terraces, waterfalls and lily ponds in the woodland areas.

The late John Barnes, son of the school's founder, bequeathed 'Ashmeadow', as a listed building, to a trust - The Barnes Trust - for the benefit of the residents of Arnside. The Trust is a group of family members and village resident friends who were chosen, personally, by John Barnes, to represent the community as a whole. He was a passionate environmentalist and ornithologist and it was hoped that the Trust could, in some way, reflect his cares and interests by the rebirth of the estate to the benefit of the residents of Arnside.

School swimming pool at Ashmeadow c.1930

The interior of the house still retains some interesting decorative features though the ravages of neglect, damp and time have not helped. Possibly the most interesting feature is the main staircase with its original Georgian, decorative metal supports to the handrail, incorporating elephant's head symbols. The latter were presumably some indication of Berry's interest in importing cargoes from the East. The oval window above the stair well is substantially intact with its coloured glass panels. Some of the cornices are also of interest but in need of repair.

There has been great difficulty in realising the terms of John Barnes bequest. After twelve years, the Trust, for lack of finance, has still failed to bring the building back into satisfactory occupation. The Trust's hopes were somewhat dashed when a tenant, The Rural Heritage Trust, went into receivership in 2001. It was, however, able to make progress in acquiring and opening out the substantial garden and woodland areas to the rear of the property. The latter were opened to public access, in 2000, to provide a number of delightful woodland walks. Here can be found two memorial seats and the school's, old boys, War Memorial dedicated in 1949 to those of their fellows who died in the two World Wars, some 20 in all.

A path, to the estuary side of 'Ashmeadow', follows the wall round. The wall gradually rises until, after about 100 metres, near the bend, it is too high to look over. A small portion of the wall, here, is of different construction and surmounted by vertical stones. At this point it was said that a boat was driven through the wall by the force of a storm. The more plausible account is that the boat, owned by the then occupant of the house, Thomas Rodick (Junior), was wrecked in the Bay. Being useless as a sailing vessel, it was converted into a summerhouse, or gazebo, giving fine estuary views. The path, of course, did not exist at that time. The boat remained in position for possibly 30 or 40 years, probably only being removed in the time of Pyke Wilson, with the wall rebuilt as we now see it. Rodick had moved from 'Wood Close' to leave his brother, Robert Preston Rodick, in occupancy.

Behind the wall, at the west end, lies the school's, old pool. Sadly the pool is not in use being almost derelict. Efforts have been made to re-open it but money is, so far, lacking.

The shoreline path divides here, as the signpost indicates. Above the signs you will see the siren, installed in the summer of 1966, which warns of the approaching bore and incoming tide. This is a warning to sailors, walkers and fishers, of impending danger. There have been a number of drowning fatalities over the years. The estuary tides rise very powerfully and rapidly owing to the funnel nature of the shoreline. The ebb tides can be just as dangerous being even swifter with the following river flow.. The lower route, past the old boatyard shed and Coastguard Station, can often be under water at the higher tides. A narrow concrete path, beyond here, was laid by Mr. Popplewell, of 'Beachwood House', in 1952. It now provides access to the Beachwood Nature Reserve behind the sea wall. This was originally Mr. Popplewell's orchard but is now owned by the Parish Council,

Beach off Ashmeadow c. 1914

Of the two upper routes, which both lead up on to Redhills Road, that to the left was the original access route to the boatyard, for timber and materials. The path to the right, past the little café, has been a public footpath for about a century. The café, itself, would appear to have been there since the 1920s and the heydays of Arnside as a holiday resort. The newer, 1980's house, up to the right beyond the café, replaces 'Dungarth' a late 19th century house that suffered severe fire damage in 1956.

No longer in use, the boatyard shed, here, was the final destination of the Crossfield boat building enterprises in Arnside. When the original family business in Church Hill was split, this yard was developed by William Crossfield, under the name 'William Crossfield and Sons', in 1893. The original, single storey workshop had a hipped roof. A forward, doorway extension was added in 1900 to accommodate the longer boats. The superstructure and lookout room are a relatively modern addition. Although bought over in the 1950s, the yard passed through several hands only to close completely in the early 1990s. Its future is now in doubt, one of the additional sheds already having been replaced by the new Coastguard Station. Suffice to say that this small yard was responsible for launching some of the finest Morecambe Bay shrimpers and small craft, at the hands of the Crossfield Brothers and successors, for over 80 years. A model of the business is to be found in the Lancaster Maritime Museum together with some of the tools and wooden patterns used in shaping the cross-members. The museum also preserves two original boats from the Crossfield yard.

The Boat-Builder Crossfields (1838 - 1951)

The family firm, later to split in two, soon established a reputation for the excellence of its sailing craft and kept many members, of the increasing family, in work. (Thomas and Francis fathered 7 sons who married to increase the families resident, in the village, in the late 19th century) Arnside was to see this firm launch many of the Morecambe Bay shrimpers, small yachts and dinghies, for a century, before it finally closed and passed on to others.

With the opening of the railway station, Arnside began to grow, as did building and traffic along this part of the front. As a result the boat-yard and building workshops moved up into a road behind the shops, Church Hill. They are still there but now occupied by a joinery and undertaking business continuing a part of the original Crossfield business.

Towards the end of the century, in 1893, the premises proved to be too small to cope with all the business available so a new yard was established along the shore, on land bought from John Matthias Barker of 'Saltcotes', and the business divided between three sets of Crossfield relatives, operating in the two locations. William and his two sons, Frederick (Fred) John and Francis, established themselves at the new foreshore yard as 'William Crossfield & Sons'.

George Crossfield and his sons, Herbert and another George, together with brother John and his sons, Francis, Alfred and Vincent, carried on the business in Church Hill as 'Crossfield Brothers'. It was almost certainly the latter group that

Last of the Arnside Crossfield boat-builders, Francis and Frederick c. 1950

was involved with house building at the end of the century. Plans were drawn up and submitted by the firm but it is most likely that they were only involved with the carpentry and joinery of the actual building. This would account for the number of family members involved. Some would be outworkers on construction sites around the village. About 1903, John and family, apart from Francis, moved away to Conway (Conwy). George died in 1909 but his two sons carried on a, much reduced, business, repairing and hiring out boats and acting as the local undertakers.

It would appear that the latter business was sold on, around the start of the First World War, leaving boat building to continue only at William's 'Beach Walk' yard. It would be around this time that the yard took on the building of power driven boats. Considering the small size of these workshops it is interesting to learn that, in their heyday, the Crossfields were producing boats of an average length of some 32 ft. (c.10 m.) overall. The largest yacht was over 38 ft. (11.6 m.) in length and the very last cutter style yacht, built in 1938, was 33 ft. in length. The majority of boats would have been shrimpers and prawners though private yachts and cruisers would be built to order. It is possible that the firm was responsible for about 1000 boats in its century of existence. The size record must go, apparently, to a 50 ft. (15.25 m.) steam yacht built by Fred Crossfield, last of the boat-builder Crossfields in Arnside, who retired after the Second World War. From then on the remaining shore yard concentrated on small boats and repair work, ownership having passed

to others such as John Gill, John Duerden, and Stanley Ogden. The yard finally closed in the late 1980s to be partly replaced later by the new Coastguard Station. The original, modified, 1893 building remains but is currently in a sorry state.

The new Coastguard Station was opened in 1995, replacing a large shed, developed as part of the post-war boatyard. The rock formations hereabouts will be of some interest to the geologist. The small quarry was, no doubt, used to obtain much of the building stone; hewn here, and hauled up the cliff to build the older houses lying, out of sight, at the top.

The quarry, with its unsightly stub concrete walls, was used as a boat park and, in the 19th and early 20th centuries, was probably used in connection with the annual sailing regattas. The original foreshore 'Coronation' shelter of 1903 was here for many years, near the flagstaff base, which can still be seen. The shelter was moved to the Lower Promenade, site of the old Customs House, in the 1920s but since re-built.

The beach here is usually known as Beachwood Beach, being so-named after the Victorian 'Beachwood House' which lies behind the sea wall, further to the west. A little beyond the quarry, along the narrow concrete path, is a small flight of steps in the wall. Behind the wall here, lies the small, but interesting, Beachwood Nature Reserve. Originally an orchard, the reserve was given to the Parish Council in June 1966. Notice the tall conifers and the variety of flora hereabouts. Looking over the wall there are fine view of the estuary across to Meathop, Ulpha and Grange-over-Sands with the hills of the Lake District as a backdrop. Tides, in the estuary, rise and fall very quickly. At the highest spring tides, the water will lap high against this wall.

Oak Mount c. 1904

On the other side of the path, beyond the two joined modern houses alongside the Reserve, is a house with stone columns, facing on to the estuary. Built originally in 1777 as 'Pear Tree Cottage', and, then, serving as an inn, it was a home for a branch of the Saul family who lived in a farm at the top of this lane. It was bought by Thomas Rodick (Senior), in 1849, enlarged and renamed 'Beechwood'. Rodick, a retired Liverpool banker, J.P. and a Deputy-Lieutenant for Lancashire, had moved here from 'Wood Close'.

Extended over the years, the building is now split into several dwellings. Principal developer was John Crossley who bought the house and 85-acre estate on the death of Thomas Rodick, in 1874. He was responsible for considerable additions and the creation of several smaller dwellings for servants together with a coach-house, up the hill. It was Crossley who changed the name 'Beechwood' to 'Beachwood'. A path led down from Redhills Road, through the orchard across the narrow path here, by a wooden bridge, to meet the serpentine drive. Being rotten the bridge was removed in 1977. The house was originally surrounded by gardens and orchards and included large greenhouses, of which most still survive.

After the First World War the house was occupied by John Popplewell, a wealthy, Yorkshire businessman, owner of the, then, 'Thrift Store' chain. A somewhat unique family-grave headstone is to be seen in Arnside Cemetery. Incorporating cricket themes, it is the grave of a son, with a passionate interest in cricket, who died in his early twenties. Following the death of Mr. Popplewell, the estate was put up for auction in May 1964. Part of the estate came into the hands of Matson Ground Estates for

Beachwood House c. 1947

subsequent partial development of the houses and bungalows of Upper Beachwood. Some 40 acres of the estate land, on The Knott, passed to ownership of the National Trust at this time.

A WORD OF WARNING

When the tide is out, the apparently dry sands look very inviting but, here and there, they trap the unwary as quicksands. To walk out to the middle of the estuary is to tempt fate. It can be done but it really requires the expertise of the 'Queen's Guide to the Sands' for safe conduct. Walking crossings are organised during the summer months but, be warned, the distance can be seven or eight miles, according to the state of the river channels that change from day to day.

RED HILLS

Higher up the narrow, concreted path are several old, stone properties lying close to the original, gated entrance to the Beachwood estate on the right, and which were, themselves, a part of it. The larger, detached, 'Hillside Cottage' was the butler's residence. Semi-detached 'Yew Tree Cottage' and 'Beachwood Cottage' were servants' houses, the former incorporating the laundry in a, then, multi-chimneyed extension, to the rear. Investigation showed that these two cottages were the result of an early barn conversion. Opposite is the old coach-house with quarters for the coachman and groom. The centre archway entrance has been used to provide a further, small, infill cottage.

At the top of Beachwood Lane is Redhills Road. The building and grounds on the far, east side, here, are the premises of 'Parkside Guest House'. This is a popular holiday venue for walking parties or for the more elderly who like the on-the-spot entertainment with dancing, games, a bowling green and a putting green. Until the 1950's, they were part of a private boarding school for girls - Oakfield School which, outgrowing its premises in Arnside, moved to Kirkby Lonsdale.

OAKFIELD SCHOOL 1884-1959

Started on Arnside front at 'Earnseat' (now 'Tankerfield') in 1884 by Mrs. Mary Proctor, with around 12 pupils, the school was firmly established at 'Oakfield House', with 18 pupils, by 1891. By this time both Mr and Mrs. Proctor were teaching helped by two further assistant teachers. There were also three domestic staff. The pupils came from as far away as Hull, Durham, Keighley and even Cornwall.

This house now forms the front part of the present building but was originally known as 'Ivy Cottage' a part of Lawrence House Farm next door. In 1895, 'Oakfield School', as it had then become known, was acquired by the Rev. J.M. Bamford and his family, which included his son, the Rev. G.H. Bamford with his wife and three daughters.

The two elder daughters, Helen and Kate, assumed responsibility for the teaching while the youngest, Millie, helped their mother with the domestic side of this small boarding school. In 1902 the school became a centre for the sitting of Cambridge Examinations and in 1904 a centre for musical examinations of the Associated Board of the Royal Academy and Royal College of Music. Helen married in 1904 and moved away with her husband, F.W. Gamble. Brother Dr. Herbert Gamble, F.R.S. was a schoolmaster who became the Head of the Scholastic side of the school following marriage to Helen's sister, Kate.

The school, in common with its boys' equivalent at 'Earnseat', offered a wide academic curriculum together with a range of outdoor activities on its own playing fields and courts. Hockey, lacrosse, cricket and tennis were standard sports at one period or another. 'Earnseat' beat 'Oakfield' at cricket by 100 runs to 24, in the summer of 1905. Joint activities were often organised with the boys' school and, indeed, Mr. J.A. Barnes shared the teaching of environmental subjects, in the school, with Dr. Ganble. It is recorded that the latter gave a copy of Hudson's 'British Birds' to the library. A Mr. Roscoe, possibly the later village Methodist Minister (1918 - 1922), presented the school with a torch.

Outgrowing the house, the school expanded into other properties along the road such as 'Heathcliffe' and the adjoining 'Haslemere'. 'New Oakfield' (now the Y.H.A.) was built as an extension from about 1911. Even the old 'Dungarth', on

Oakfield School c. 1910

Shady Bower (a sloping path down to the shore), was used for accommodation at one period. The elder Mr. Bamford died in 1916. In the same year Mr. and Mrs. Gamble moved to Surbiton and Millie, the youngest of the sisters, became Head of the School with Miss Eacott, teacher and ex-pupil, as deputy. This successful partnership ended when both retired in 1935 to be succeeded by Miss Birnie Rhind.

The school continued to develop and prosper under the guidance of Miss Birnie Rhind until she, too, retired in 1949 whereupon the school was taken over by the Methodist Church Society. With Miss Ethel Randle as Head, the school became officially recognised as a minor Public School having moved to Underley Hall, at Kirkby Lonsdale, in 1945. The Church Society acquired Luckley School in Wokingham in 1959. Founded in 1918, this was another successful girls' school and it was decided to combine the two schools on the Luckley House site. Thus in September 1959 the schools came together as the Luckley-Oakfield School for Girls, under the headship of Miss Randle and with a combined total of 90 boarding pupils. Miss Randle eventually retired, in 1969, but the school still goes on from strength to strength as a member of the Headmistresses' Conference. So the second of the two most successful schools, in Arnside, still plays a part in history.

Parkside Drive houses, to the right, are built on what were the playing fields and orchards of the school. The original 'Oakfield House', and its on-site extensions, was to become the present 'Parkside Guest House' and a member of the Grey Court Fellowship group. 'New Oakfield' was taken over as a private house, until the 1970s, when it was sold on to the Y.H.A., ultimately to become one of its flagship hostels.

To the more-northerly side of the guesthouse is a white-painted cottage-type house on the corner of Lawrence Drive. This is 'Lawrence House', rebuilt and modernised in recent years but originally an 18th Century farmhouse with a barn built-in at the rear and known, in the early 19th century, as 'Granny House'. It was bought by a John Saul probably around 1770. The farm was occupied for well over a century by a branch of the Saul family, and, for almost 70 years more, by descendants. Last of the Sauls here were Robert Saul and his wife, Ann, who had moved from 'Ivy Cottage' next door. Life as a working farm diminished with loss or sale of land. From around 1900 Ann Saul, by then widowed, and son William Washington Saul were principally concerned in the running of a carting and carriage business. The Washington name was due to connections with the Washingtons of Warton who in turn had distant connections with George Washington. It appears again with another relative by marriage, George Washington Edgar, who died in 1990 aged 87. The Saul connection seems to have ended with the death, in 1967 aged 92, of Anne Willacy, a daughter of Robert Saul. Before 1800, the Saul families owned a large proportion of this corner of Beetham Parish. For one reason or another this ownership was gradually whittled away during the 19th Century and there are, seemingly, no Sauls in Arnside at the present day though a number of descendants in the Willacy, Edgar, Taylor, and other lines, remain.

The nearby tree stump, apparently known locally as 'Old Oak', was in the farmyard and is the remains of a splendid oak, cut down because of honey fungus in the early 1990s. The stump has a ring count indicating an age of some 300 years. This small piece of land was given to the Parish Council, by owner and local developer, L. Woodburn, in 1979.

The Saul connection is retained in the three houses of Saul Gardens, which are built on land originally part of 'Lawrence House Farm'. Prior to development, in the late 1980s, this had been the site of the Redhills Garden Centre, with several large greenhouses. The latter had, in turn, been acquired from Mr. Norman Rathbone who had lived in, what is now, the Y.H.A. building, opposite. A keen gardener in younger days, he had often supplied the church with flowers.

The early developments of the late 1800s took place on the estuary side of Redhills Road, largely because of the magnificent views. 'Oakmount', the stone house opposite the pillar-box, became another boarding school for boys, opened in 1921. The headmaster was Mr Gillman, who, succeeded by his wife in 1916, had been head of

New Oakfield c 1920

Arnside National School from 1913. In the intervening period, prior to opening the new school with his wife, he had taught at Lancaster Royal Grammar School. The school closed in 1941.

As already mentioned the attractive stone building, with the round, 'Westmorland' style chimneys, was built as an extension to Oakfield School, about 1911, and, appropriately, called 'New Oakfield'. A private residence for some years, it has been a 'flagship' Youth Hostel, since 1977, and renamed 'Oakfield Lodge'.

The next building was built, towards the end of the last century, as large, semi-detached houses - 'Heathcliffe' and 'Haslemere'. Both housed private schools at times, either as extensions to 'Oakfield' or as independents. 'Heathcliffe' housed 'Westholme School', principal Miss Fowler, from 1945 to 1953, after Oakfield School had moved. 'Haslemere' was a school for boys. Continuing the Methodist connection, established by the Reverend Bamford, owner of 'Oakfield House' and a founder of the girls' school, the two houses were later linked and converted into flats for retired ministers, after the schools had closed. Sold on in 1990, the building was doubled in size and developed into 16 superior, modern flats with an underground car park. It suffered two serious roof fires during the development, in 1990.

The next old house, again apartments and surrounded by small bungalows, was a private dwelling called 'Brantfell'. It was built for a Kendal solicitor, Henry Thompson, together with the previously mentioned 'Dungarth', about 1882. Living initially in 'Brantfell' he was, about 1898, to move into 'Dungarth' where he died in 1908. For a few years the house was occupied by the Gambles, teachers at Oakfield School. It was eventually leased and occupied, in 1914, by the Heath family. The house was bought in 1917 and the property enhanced by the purchase of the coppice below the garden, in 1921. In recent years the coppice has been acquired by the Woodland Trust. Mrs. Heath was a founder member of the Arnside Women's Institute in 1919, and, possibly, some of the first few meetings were held in this house. As President, Mrs. Heath was largely instrumental in procuring the development of the W.I. Hall in 1928. In 1934 the property was purchased by Robert ('Robin') Sands Crossfield a member of the Timber Merchant branch of the family in Barrow. Now an Abbeyfield Home, 'Brantfell' was renamed 'Crossfield House' by benefactor and late occupant, Mrs. Miriam Crossfield, widow of R.S. Crossfield, O.B.E., D.L. Mr. Crossfield was another prominent and eminent 20th century member of the Crossfield family, sometime Chairman of Parish, District and Westmorland County Councils, and High Sheriff of Westmorland (1970-71). A ring of 6 oak saplings (The Crossfield Circle) was planted in 1981 in Redhills Wood in memory of Mr. Crossfield. Mrs. Crossfield died in October 2001 aged 92.

'Beechmount' (originally 'Beachmount') next door, and not so readily seen as the front faces the estuary, is actually a terrace of three large houses with a low cottage butting on to the end, dating from around 1875. The cottage was probably an example of a dame school. Now a private dwelling, it is certainly recorded as a school in 1900.

Uplands House c. 1905

Beyond a small row of modern bungalows, is the entry to another, now rather hidden, large, Victorian house called 'Uplands'. The older building on the roadside, was its coach-house and servants' quarters. The grounds have been developed with bungalows and the roadside buildings converted to houses.

Apart from two large, semi-detached, Edwardian houses of about 1908, most of the properties on the footpath side of the road, here, are of little historical significance, dating largely from the 1930's. They are all developments on what was known in the village as 'The Common'. Owner Mr. Bradley-Barker of 'Saltcotes', having had his sale offer to the Parish Council turned down, proceeded to build on the land, much to the annoyance of many. The land had been used for fetes, school sports, celebration events and the like for many years.

About 100 metres further on, is an apparently windowless, barn-like building on the corner of the entrance to the Inglemeres' estate. This old building, again a converted lodge and coach house (1978), is all that remains of what must have been, in Victorian period development, the largest building in Arnside. This was the site of 'Inglemere House', built about 1872 for R.F. Thompson, yet another solicitor. It was probably the first development of substance on this Red Hills plateau. Redhills gets its name from the presence of red iron ore in the underlying limestone rock. 'Inglemere' was purchased at auction in 1908, greatly extended and, from 1911, used as a new home for another boarding school for girls, established in 1905 and thence to be known as 'Inglemere School for Girls'. The Headmistress, at this time, was Mrs. Llewellyn wife of the Principal of 'Aylwin College for Boys' on High Knott Road. In the 1943

Inglemere School for Girls c. 1912

it became a guesthouse with Mr. & Mrs. Nicholson as proprietors. Later, with the help of their unmarried daughter it became 'The Inglemere Hotel' with its own farm and large ornamental gardens. Sadly, circumstances led to its sale and demolition, in 1968, to be replaced by the present houses and bungalows of the Inglemeres Estate and the retirement flats of 'Millom Court' (1974). One or two of the bungalows still retain some of the cellars of the old house as substructures. The lodge is now converted to two attractive houses but they can only be admired from the other side.

A field to the right, here at the High Knott Road junction, gives pleasant views along its length to the backdrop of the woods behind. An attractive field footpath, one of the oldest in the village, leads along the lower fringe of the wood to, eventually, The Knott. The field still generally known as 'The Common', but not legally common land, is now merely grazing land currently protected from development for its scenic or 'amenity' value. It was offered to the Parish Council, in 1903, for about half its value at £2,000 but turned down for lack of funds. Referred to as the 'Recreation Field' by its then owner, Mr. R. Bradley-Barker, it was 6_ acres in area with a value of 2/6 per sq.yard. An opportunity missed! The field was used for many years for Sports Days and Gala Events by the various boarding schools in the village.

High Knott Road rises to a higher plateau, or belvedere, with a mixed group of Victorian, Edwardian, and later houses having attractive views up the estuary. Older properties, here, developed around the turn of the 19th century. One was the site of

High Knott Road houses c. 1930

yet another boys' school and companion to that for girls, at 'Inglemere'. This was 'Aylwin College', started in Church Hill in 1902 at Greenwood House, by a Mr. Llewellyn and moving up here in 1904. Working in partnership with the girls' school it was able to claim having its own farm. School Principal was Mr. W.K. Innes, a Cambridge graduate. It had an annexe built on to its Eastern end about 1910. This eventually connected the main house to a new set of classrooms, which today remain only as semi-detached houses - 'The Shielings' and 'Deveron'. The joining annexe was pulled down about 1928, probably when the college closed, and transferred to 'Ashmeadow' to be re-erected as a gymnasium, there. With the potential opening up of the 'Ashmeadow' gardens, it was demolished in 1998. For many years a private residence, the house is now divided as two large family semi-detached houses.

Most houses here are large individual dwellings though the two earliest are now mainly converted to apartments. The nursing home at the western end, 'Westmorland Court' (previously 'Redlands'), was originally large semi-detached houses used as boarding houses. That at the end was called 'Ulriksdal', about 1910. Close by, at 'Sunny Bank', now 'Windrush', there was a small orphanage established at about the same time as the college. Under the ownership of Miss Wishaw in 1902, and recorded yet again in 1909, it does not appear to have survived very long. The 'Oakfield (School) Magazine' records a charity donation of 7/6d. as a "Christmas Gift to the Children in Miss Wishaw's Home". Originally one large house built in 1898 it was divided in 1902 into semis. The adjacent house, then, had the strange name of 'The Bobolinks'! A Dr. Till ran a maternity home at 'The Chase' around the time of the Second World War. The woodland area to the west of 'Westmorland Court' has been deprived of

some of its natural beauty by felling of trees. The name 'Dobbs Hall' has no historical significance, it being merely a corruption derived from that of nearby Dobshall Wood, to the west. In the 1980s it was known as 'Dobshall Farm' raising pigs.

The houses near the end of Redhills Road were to be associated with 'Inglemere School' and 'Aylwin College'. They appear to have been extra dormitory accommodation for the periods of the schools and partly staff accommodation, later, for the guesthouse and hotel. 'Kingswood' dates from about 1902 and was, probably, in the late 1930s and the 1940s, a private maternity home known as 'Trerose'. The large, older 'semis', in the little cul-de-sac, were built about 1925. The large, new, detached house, opposite, is a 2001 introduction. Originally, this was to have been Kings Drive with a possible intent of a further extension that never materialised.

UPPER SILVERDALE ROAD, THE TOWER AND FAR ARNSIDE

Around the turn of the century, there were no buildings on Silverdale Road between 'Springfield' and 'Heatherlea'. Orchard Road, initially here a cul-de-sac known as Meadow Street, with the Meadowbank terrace of houses, did not exist. 'Heatherlea' was, at one period, used as accommodation for 'Earnseat School'. The Playing Field, originally known as 'Big King Field', belongs to the Parish Council and is dedicated as a 'Memorial Field' to those who died in war in the 20th century. It was purchased from the Bradley-Barkers for £2,000, through the agency of the King George V National Memorial Fund, in 1936.

Our Lady of Lourdes Catholic Church moved here from its Pier Lane building in 1977 following much voluntary effort by Catholic parishioners to effect the conversion and redecoration. Its new premises were originally the 1880 Sunday School of St. James's Parish Church, built on a part of Low King Field. It was to become the Church National School, opening on the 30th of August 1886 and remaining here until 1971. Before this time, children had attended the school at Beetham, walking across the marshes and over the 'scarps' at the Fairy Steps in Underlaid Wood or, for the previous twelve years, attended the fee-charging 'British School' school in Briery Bank, of which more later. Schooling would, no doubt, have been spasmodic, considering the distance; the vagaries of the weather; the state of the paths; and the need to help at harvest times. Noted and greatly esteemed, by both parents and pupils, were two head teachers, Mr. Lindsay (1917 to 1954) and Mr. Bryan (1954 to 1971).

Map evidence indicates that a blacksmith was established in a building off Park View behind the school. It is possible that this was taken over by Mr. Procter to garage his taxis, hearse and coal lorry.

There was little early development to this south end of the village apart from what now appear to be odd isolated examples. The Vicarage and adjacent 'Shawleigh' were built about 1872, rather higher up. Strangely the former was quite a distance from the church and was only relinquished for the present Vicarage in 1972. On the right, 'The Birks' was a hotel for many years up to the 1970s. Just below the road entrance, here, is a small, dilapidated building that was the first village, automatic, telephone exchange. This was later superseded by the larger building at the top of

Sunday School of 1880, National School 1886 to 1971

Briery Bank although, with the rapid developments of technology, it is only partly used. Houses on either side, beyond 'Shawleigh', largely date from the mid-1920s with a few more modern infill dwellings of later date. Four houses at the top corner of Hollins Lane date from the late 1990s.

Yet further from the village centre were the developments of Mount Pleasant and Lynslack Terrace; cottages built on lanes at right angles to the main road and on relatively small plots of land, probably by the Crossfields. Some of these seem to be examples of Victorian, low-cost housing, possibly built for quarry workers, craft and agricultural labourers or railway gangers. In the late 1920s one of the larger houses accommodated Miss Scott's, 'Mount Pleasant Preparatory School' (for Girls and little Boys !). Built towards the end of the nineteenth century, these houses and terraced, but individual, cottages would have been quite isolated from the rest of the village. A little hamlet, at the 'top' of the village, almost half way between the hamlet of Heathwaite and the river front, by The Albion!

Behind Mount Pleasant lie the relatively modern houses and bungalows of The Spinney and Spinney Lane dating from the 1970s to the end of the century.

The beginnings of Lynslack Terrace and Mount Pleasant c. 1900

The Cemetery, with its tiny chapel, was opened at the top of the village, in 1902. Previous burials had been at either Beetham or Silverdale. Until about 1990, a circular reservoir header tank for the village lay behind the wall opposite the cemetery. With new developments it could not cope with village needs and was replaced by a much larger, underground reservoir higher up in Redhills Wood.

The adjacent 'Meadows' housing development was started in the late 1980s following earlier controversy and a public enquiry referring to the density of development. Sandwiched in between the houses, here, are the Parish Council allotments. Stewart Close was the last council housing development in Arnside. Several of the houses are now in private ownership as is the case in the other council, post-war, late 1950s developments of Queens Drive and Kings Close.

There were only two other, early, developments of note. One was 'Stoneycroft', a large house on land between Silverdale Road and Briery Bank, built in 1879. This was designed and built, as a retirement home, by Thomas William Worsdell, a Quaker and well reputed, innovative, railway locomotive, design engineer from Crewe. The house was one of the first in the village to be lit with acetylene lamps. Retiring and living in the village from 1890 until his death in 1916, he was elected as the first president of the Ratepayers and Property Owners Association and, later, was active on Arnside's first elected Parish Council. He brought some of the first motorcars into the area and sailed on the estuary, owning several boats, including both a steam launch and a diesel launch.

The second development, about 100 metres down Briery Bank from Silverdale Road, on the right, is a somewhat unusual residence called, simply, 'The Cottage'. Here, in 1874, a 'British School' was established largely by the efforts of Thomas Whinray living at 'Hill House Farm' on the opposite side of Briery Bank. (At this time the Whinrays had 10 children of whom 7 were of school age !) These were independent, fee-paying schools of the Victorian era. The distance of the nearest school, at Beetham, and the poor access, prompted this initiative. In the evenings, the school was used for meetings and lectures and the beginnings of a form of adult education. Dependent on fees and donations, the school got into difficulties and eventually closed in 1886. The 37 pupils moved to the new church school. By exchange in 1887, the trustees were able to acquire premises in Pier Lane and to establish the 'Arnside Educational Institute', which opened, there, in 1888.

Briery Bank was, around 1900, known as Burton Road. It was then flanked by Whinrays' farm on the north side and orchards, fields and wood plantations, established by Robert Bush, later of 'The Albion', to the south. In the middle of the 19th century it had been known as Hollins Lane, a name that was to be resurrected, in the later 20th century, for the connecting link to Silverdale Road.

'Hill House Farm' was, for many generations, the home of the Whinray family. In the 19th and 20th centuries, families were large and some diversification required, to sustain income. Here the Whinrays established what might be described as an early marine store, or chandlery, supplying the shipping trade plying up and down the estuary. Farmed, latterly, by the Lemon family, the properties and land were split

Hill House Farm c. 1922

High Black Dyke Farm c. 1922

following the death of Mrs. Lemon. In 1999, a plot fronting Briery Bank was used to build a block of affordable houses, thereby blocking the original, attractive view of the farm. Other plots were sold on, for eventual possible redevelopment in the later 2000s, despite attempts by the community to get the land into the hands of those who would wish to preserve the area for its attractive landscape value.

Lower down, Hollins Lane on the right was, earlier, known as Hollins Road. For a period, it was called Smithy Lane as a blacksmith, Mr. Douthwaite, had his workshop on the lower corner where a bungalow now stands. As might be expected, there were several smiths in the village at a time when horsepower was paramount and farm equipment rapidly developing.

Two early communities were those of Low Black Dyke farm, near the level crossing, and High Black Dyke farm opposite the lower end of Briery Bank and nearer to the village centre. These farms both seem to have been occupied by various members of the Saul family and their relatives in the 18th and 19th centuries. From their positions it is likely that one or other of these farms could pre-date even 17th century 'Saltcotes', built by yet other Sauls. The Black Dyke, itself, originates below Arnside Tower and eventually flows into Leighton Beck behind the station. Just four houses lie beyond the level crossing. That next to the crossing housed the crossing gates keeper. The gates were to be replaced in the late 1980s by the existing remote controlled arm and lights system. A modern bungalow, beyond the dyke, is separated from two somewhat older semi-detached houses by the entry to a commercial bush and tree nursery, which was to develop and move away, in the 1990s, to be based in Carnforth as Ashlea Landscaping Ltd. About 100 metres beyond here is the bridge over Leighton Beck, which forms the civil parish boundary with Beetham.

Black Dyke Road was originally called Low Road. It was realigned, and renamed, when Sandside Road bridge was widened to permit the passage of larger vehicles such as the new (1912) motor charabancs.. The large, Victorian, 1895 development of four houses, known as 'Fairy Terrace', was originally called 'Fairy Mount'. No doubt both names refer to the fact that the Fairy Steps, in Underlaid Wood, about a mile to the north-east, would have been visible before the trees grew too high, as now.

We must now move back to the southern boundary of the village just beyond the cemetery on Silverdale Road. Some half a mile beyond here, can be found Arnside Tower and Tower Farm. The 15th century tower, often described as a 'pele' tower, is more likely to have been more of a fortified house as, normally, pele towers do not have living accommodation and fire-places at the ground floor level but do include a well. Nothing certain is known about the tower's builder. Largely built from local limestone it is suggested that some small parts are red sandstone brought by sea from as far as the Furness Abbey area. Following the battle of Bosworth Field in the late 15th century, the tower and surrounding lands passed from the 'de Beethams' to become an estate and home of the Stanleys, Earls of Derby. During the Civil War the lands were forfeit once again only to be restored to the Stanleys by Charles II, at the Restoration. It suffered a fire in 1602 and, despite some 17th century rebuilding, partly fell down in the 1884 as the result of a violent storm. It remains as Arnside's oldest listed building. It is likely that some of the tower stone was used to build the present farmhouse in the early 1700s. Middlebarrow Woods, the Tower, the farm and much of the land round about were bought from the Stanleys by Daniel Wilson of Dallam Tower in 1815. Most of this land still belongs to the Dallam Estate.

Concealed from this north side, in Middlebarrow Wood beyond the Tower, lies Middlebarrow Quarry. The worked out quarry has recently been left back to nature after more than 120 years of limestone extraction. It will remain a vast, but potentially dangerous, hole in the ground 'protecting' the counties' boundary. It is unlikely to be open to the public. The boundary wall of the quarry and the wood, to the south, marks the boundary between Cumbria and Lancashire. It is unfortunate that the modern postal system gives many Cumbrian villages seemingly Lancastrian addresses. History, however, shows that the counties' boundary was established as far back as the 12th century. The whole of Arnside Parish, including Far Arnside, lies within the Westmorland part of modern Cumbria. Thus Holgates Caravan Parks and the Leeds Children's Holiday Camp are in Cumbria but have Silverdale (Lancashire) postal addresses.

In the mid-19th century 'Tower Farm' close by, was the home of Robert Gibson, Methodist lay-preacher, who, moving into the area from Langdale, reinforced Methodism in Arnside and district. With the nearest Methodist chapel some way away in Silverdale, he held services at the farm. These would be outdoors in fair

Arnside Tower Farm and Arnside Tower c. 1916

conditions, but in a barn or in the farm kitchen if the weather was really bad. The farm was probably built around 1700 from the ruins of the Tower though it is possible that an earlier farm existed to service the families who once occupied the Tower. In the 20th century the farm has largely been occupied by two farming families - the Robinsons and, latterly, the Blands. At one time the small beck and pond below the farm were a commercial source of watercress. The farm is now mainly concerned with sheep and some dairy cattle and is also the centre for the distribution of the local milk supplies.

The hamlet to the west of 'Tower Farm', and south of The Knott, is known as Far Arnside, though still a part of Arnside Parish. It would appear that before 1850 there were probably more people living here than in the main village. The southern aspect would have encouraged farming and accounted for other farms such as 'Hollins' and 'Arnside Well'. The latter has long since disappeared so that the only remnant is 'Priory Cottage' to indicate its whereabouts. It was certainly occupied by a Thomas Rawlinson in 1800. On the shoreline, near the present caravan site, there were a number of fishermen's cottages of which only traces remain. Here also are traces of an old 'rope walk' used to supply ropes for repair work on boats anchored out in the estuary. During the two World Wars, part of the beach was used as a rifle range by soldiers camping and training in the area. The substantial nature of some of the remaining old properties, here, would seem to indicate the existence of odd smallholdings or trades such as blacksmith or stonemason. There is also suggestion of a leather worker in the area. Although now referred to as Far Arnside this settlement was earlier known as Heathwaite a name now only associated with the National Trust land close by.

Leeds Children's Holiday Camp c. 1913

Near the shore, and alongside the wall that forms the counties' boundary, lies the Leeds Children's Holiday Camp. Opened in June of 1905, with a grand civic reception, as The Leeds Poor Children's Holiday Camp, it has been in regular use ever since. The original building was largely destroyed in a disastrous fire in 1919. Nowadays, as seems to be the fashion, the land in front is often used for car-boot sales.

At this point, the boundary walls, on either side of the road, delineate the ancient limits of the counties of Lancashire and Westmorland. With the administarive changes of 1974, the boundary is now that of Lancashire and Cumbria. Thus Arnside is one of the southernmost and largest villages, by population, of modern Cumbria.

Today, Far Arnside is better known for the Holgate and Far Arnside caravan sites. Well laid out, serviced and organised, they must be regarded as a credit to the Holgate family which now owns both. The site acquired a brand new swimming pool, shop, bar and café complex, in 1999. The latter, open to all, can provide an excellent cup of tea, and other refreshments at reasonable prices, to the weary walker. There is a path across the fields to 'Hollins Farm' and the National Trust land of Heathwaite, on the lower slopes of The Knott. This connects with Sauls' Drive, which, continuing over the shoulder of The Knott, eventually reaches New Barns Road close to its junction with Redhills Road and to Parkside Guest House. A second path leads to Arnside Tower and 'Tower Farm'. Paths cross the boundary, to the south, into Lancashire and the village of Silverdale

There is a footpath, round the cliffs to New Barns and Arnside village, starting from Far Arnside caravan park. It is considerably longer than the Sauls Drive route. While the route is picturesque, it is very narrow, tortuous and rough underfoot. There have been many incidents of people slipping over the cliff edge, breaking bones and

having to be rescued by boat or helicopter. It is not recommended for the less-than-active elderly or the infirm. The utmost care has to be taken in wet weather. Nevertheless it can be a most attractive path for the sure-footed.

The sand route can be easier but there are often deep pools, possible quicksands and the ever threatening rush of the tide to trap the unwary at the bottom of the cliffs. Always check the local tide tables before attemting such a venture.

Opposite the entry to Arnside Tower Farm is a gated lane and continuing path, over the shoulder of The Knott, to Arnside village. This is the same Sauls' Drive mentioned in the previous paragraph. It is so-called after the local farming family, which, at one time, owned large areas of the fields and woods to the north side of the hill.

ARNSIDE KNOTT AND NEW BARNS

The Knott 'stands guard' near the mouth of the Kent Estuary. Strangely there seems to be little evidence that its summit has been the site of any camp, fort or watchtower. The presence of numerous fortified houses and pele towers; such as Arnside Tower, Hazelslack Tower, Dallam, Levens, Sizergh, and others; would seem to indicate an expectation of incursions, by the Scots or by pirates, to the gently sloping shores of this estuary.

A large part of The Knott is now in the keeping of the National Trust as a result of gifts, or purchase using grants and public donations. Most recent acquisition, mainly through the efforts of the Parish Council and public donations, has been a large area,

The Knotted Trees c. 1920

on the south side, known as 'Heathwaite'. This mixed area of pasture and woodland is rich in wild flowers, butterflies and insects. Regular tree felling and replanting has been carried out on The Knott over the centuries. Most of the larch trees, which covered the summit area of The Knott, were felled in 1915 as part of the war effort but a good deal of coppice wood and yew trees remain.

Near the summit of The Knott, there used to be four conifer trees that had, somehow, been coupled in pairs to form what, for over a century, were known as 'The Knotted Trees'.

Various ideas have been broached as to when, by whom and how it was done but no one has come up with satisfactory answers. One pair completely rotted away in the 1980s while the other pair is now in a sorry state as the one remaining vertical trunk has been sawn off short. In 1987, Arnside resident, Mrs. Lois Marland, made an attempt to repeat the process with two young trees, close by. Success is not so easy to come by as one might imagine. Now, even these have been vandalised and disappeared.

A little higher up is a viewpoint seat dedicated to the memory of Parish Councillor H.B. Lawson who died in 1981. On the actual summit can be found the original Ordnance Survey triangulation pillar, now in the care of the, 180-strong, Arnside Ramblers Group. An engraved, stainless steel, mountain view toposcope was established on the northern face of The Knott in 1982.

Near the highest point of Sauls' Drive, approached from the village side, is the National Trust car park with a parking 'honesty box' cairn at the entrance.

The pasturelands on the lower northern slopes of The Knott were, from 1906 to 1914, the site of the, 9-hole, Arnside Golf Course. The First World War led to its closure, never to re-open. Its Secretary had been Mr. Hudson, father of local personality, organist and one-time Parish Council Chairman, Thomas ('Tommy') Hudson. There were plans in the 1974 to develop a new course lower down in the area of 'High Close' and Dobshall Wood and Field but these were turned down by the local planning authority.

For many years, until 2000, a large, art deco style building could be seen from Sauls Drive, behind the wall at the bottom of the open field. This was 'Grange View', a convalescent home belonging to the Manchester and Salford Saturday Fund.

THE CONVALESCENT HOME

This original building stemmed from small beginnings at the start of the 20th century. The first private house in the area was probably that known as 'Far Close', built, and occupied, by Thomas Wilkinson before his move to the West Promenade. It was sold at auction in 1905 and established as 'Briarfield Women's Home' in 1906. In 1928 the house was incorporated into a much larger building that became 'Briarfield Convalescent Home'. This was eventually to be taken over by the Saturday Fund.

In 1938 an extension was proposed alongside the original building. This was to be 'Grange View Convalescent Home', with a main entrance in Knott Lane. It was completed and used from 1939 but not officially opened until after the war. The older 'Briarfield' building was pulled down in the 1960s.

Popular in post-war years 'Grange View' had an additional floor added. This was opened on the 3rd April 1971 by the then Lord Mayor of Manchester, Councillor W.A. Downward. 'Grange View' suffered a serious fire in January 1977 and, as a result, was closed for several months. The home had a games room, a bowling green and attractive gardens. Its use declined in the 1990s and rarely seemed to be occupied to capacity. It was the subject for various conversion planning applications. Eventually, at the beginning of 2000, permission was granted for the demolition of this rare example of a 1930s, 'Art Deco', development comparable with the Midland Hotel in Morecambe. The 1971, top floor, additions, unfortunately, prevented its preservation as a listed building. It has been replaced, at the start of the 21st century, by the even larger block of 'The Grange', a development of 20 fashionable apartments and an abutting west-end house.

Through the bounding walls, Sauls Drive becomes Knott Lane. By the joint efforts of the Arnside Village Society and the Arnside Parish Council, the field and wood, on the east side of Knott Lane and below the extensive grounds of 'High Close', were purchased, opened to access with public donations and grants and given into the care of the Woodland Trust, in 1996. In late spring the wood, Dobshall Wood, is filled with carpets of primroses, violets and cowslips. The field is a happy feeding ground for rabbits, pheasants and the occasional deer, in the absence of any dogs.

Below 'The Grange', and westwards, lies the area of Arnside referred to as New Barns. The road to the left, New Barns Road (but originally Briarfield Road), takes the original line of the track to New Barns Farm. The farm, down on the estuary side about a kilometre further on, is one of the older established farms of the village. Like many estuary-side properties of the 18th and 19th centuries it was probably also an inn and, at Blackstone Point, there was a landing or loading point for river traffic. While practical farming has declined latterly, the farm has acquired a new crop - caravans! The trees of Frith Wood now partly conceal a large number of static caravans. At one time rather ragged, the site has got its 'act' together with almost all new, but large, vans in rather more attractive settings than hitherto. There was a suggestion of a golf driving range, happily turned down by the planners.

Frith and, adjacent, Arnside Park Woods used to be noted for their wild flowers, particularly snowdrops and wild daffodils, earlier in the century. This feature gave rise to Wilson's 'Lilyland' picture postcard series at the beginning of the 20th century. Relatively few of these blooms remain to be seen in springtime but there can be quite a little display alongside the shoreline path near Far Arnside. It was customary, in days gone by, to pick bunches of lilies of the valley and daffodils having paid the 6d. entry dues to the gamekeeper at the gate. Now, in part, Frith Wood, containing a number of old yew trees, conceals the village's sewage settling tanks that were established here as far back as 1924 and, at present, remain as the village's only sewage system. The latter is likely to be upgraded in the next few years to cope with the growth of the village. Arnside Park Wood shows small evidence of iron ore working. An Arnside mine is certainly recorded as far back as 1707 in Dallam Tower Estate papers. Presumably the project was not financially viable. Also near here, but a little off the beaten tracks, can be found the Arnside cave, much explored but seemingly of little consequence.

Much individual development has taken place along New Barns Road since about 1910. Most houses, in New Barns, were built from the 1930s on, within small cul-de-sacs off to either side. Far Close Drive rises up the side of The Knott giving magnificent views for the houses at its top end. Most of the houses here have large gardens but, in some cases, parts have been sold on to allow for further, individual plot development. One of the later developed plots at 'Oakthwaite' on the north side, was the site of the 1930s Arnside Tennis Club. At present, the old clubhouse remains as a summerhouse.

Between the gardens on the north side and the estuary shore lie Grubbins Wood and Meadow. This environmentally sensitive area is managed by the Cumbria Wildlife Trust. A part of the meadow, at the shore side, is the boat park for the Arnside Sailing Club.

Arnside has become the largest rural community in South Lakeland with little employment, now relatively poor transport services, an above average age population and a great reliance on the internal combustion engine.

The village lies in the Arnside/Silverdale Area of Outstanding Natural Beauty, designated in 1972. The A.O.N.B., is one of the smallest in the country having an area of 75 sq.km. of which some 30 sq. km. are inter-tidal. The Area, bounded by the A6 highway and the Rivers Kent, Bela and Keer, straddles the boundary of the counties of Lancashire and Cumbria. It comprises the villages of Arnside, Beetham, Silverdale, Warton, Yealand Conyers, Yealand Redmayne and Warton and the hamlets of Storth, Sandside, Hale, Hazelslack, Slack Head, Haverbrack, Yealand Storrs and Waterslack.

The designation behoved the planners to try to limit development and to afford the required environmental protection. The dangers were largely addressed in the accepted, District Local Plan of 1997, when most of the remaining large open green areas, within the defined limits of the village built-up area, were afforded protection from development as Important Areas of Amenity Value. There was some dismay in 1999 when a low-cost housing development took place on a defined area at the top of Briery Bank. Part of the distant view and sight of the old, historically important, Hill House Farm was largely lost in the process. The village residents now face the future with some trepidation. What will be the effects of the year 2000, Countryside Rights of Way Act? Will the new Local Plan of 2006 sacrifice yet more of the village's 'green lung' fields? The beauty, which attracts most people and led to the designation of the area as an Area of Outstanding Natural Beauty, is slowly but surely being whittled away.

The Landscape Trust of the A.O.N.B., together with its Countryside Management Service, attempts to look after and manage the natural environment of the area. In 1986 the Arnside Village Society was formed to keep a watchful eye on proposed planning developments. Its aims were to retain the environmental character of the village and its surroundings, to maintain a reasonable balance between its rural and urban characteristics and to oppose developments contrary to the tenets of County and Local Plans. The 21st century will see whether significantly more of the village will disappear under concrete, bricks and mortar.

If you have keeping up with new editions, you will have learned yet more about the recent history of Arnside - its residents, its buildings and its work. If you have walked the area, you will have seen something of its beauty and recognise the qualities of the natural and built-up environment which the Parish Council, the Village Society and the Landscape Trust have worked to protect and preserve. Once a noted health resort, the village is still, as for much of the latter half of the 20th century, struggling with its problems of traffic, estuary pollution and threats of further development. With time, these problems will be overcome. There is already some suggestion that a new sewage disposal system is in the planning stage. The village will survive to remain as an attractive semi-rural community.

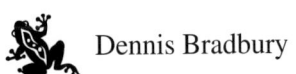

Dennis Bradbury

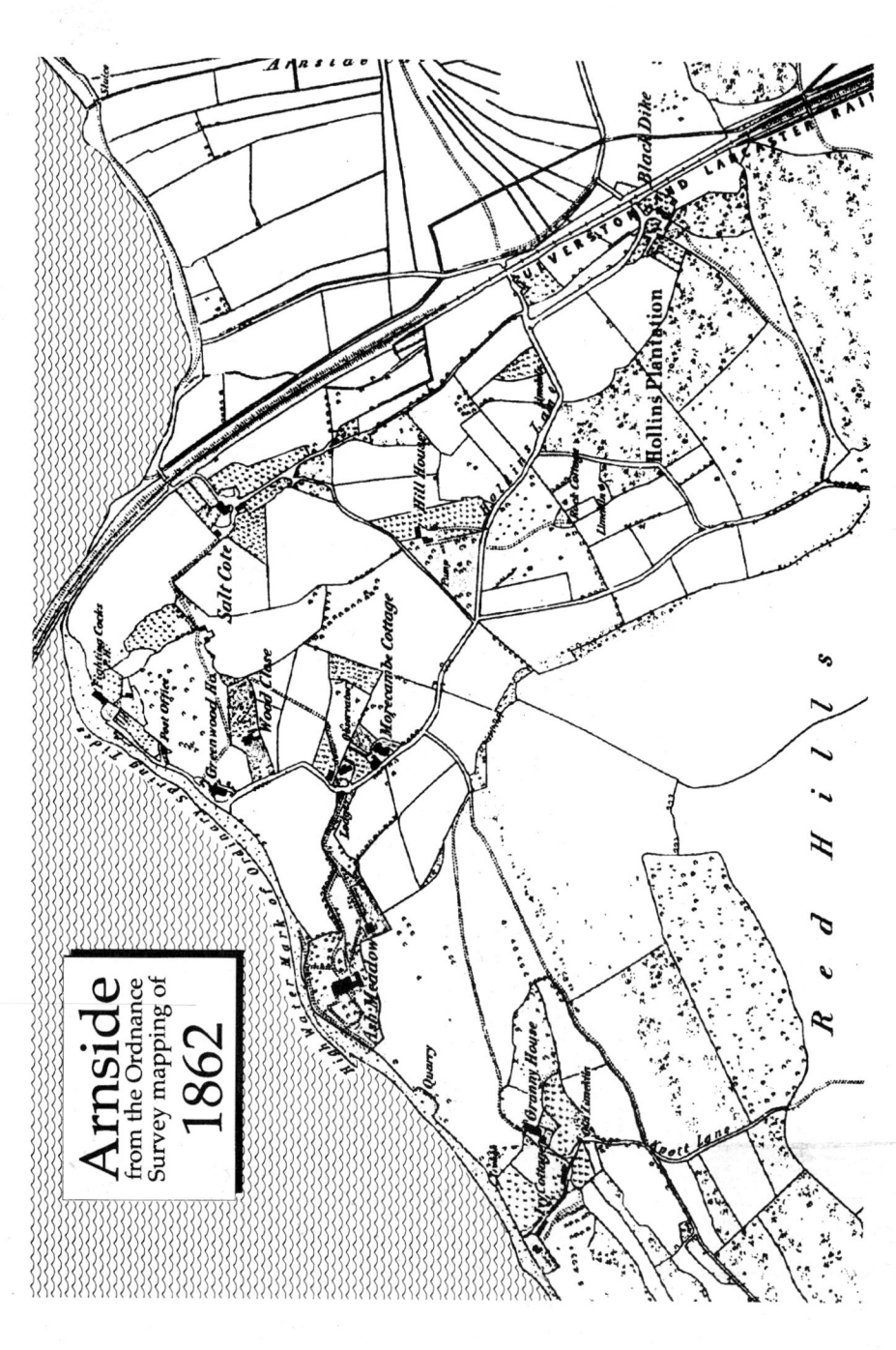